ONCE UPON A DIME,
TWO TICKS SAT,
PLANNING CRIME.
THEIR CLEVER ENDEAVOR
MUST HAVE BEEN A SNORTER
'CAUSE NOW THEY SIT
ON A SILVER QUARTER.

ANYTHIN' LESS
THAN ON A SILVER DOLLAR
IS LIVIN' ON SQUALOR.

UPWARD MOBILITY
IS OUR RESPONSIBILITY.

THESE THEM EYES
MESMERIZE.
DO NOT STARE
INTO THEM PAIR,
OR THEY'LL HAVE YOU THINK
THAT YOU ARE A MINK
FLOATING IN KITCHEN SINK

OR MAYBE A BABY BEAR
EATIN' A FORBITTEN PEAR
AN' SITTIN' ON A PINK
SQUARE, SOMEWHERE.

I AM NOT A BEAR
EATING A PEAR.
I MEAN, I AM EATING A PEAR,
BUT I AM NOT A BEAR!
I AM NOT A BEAR,
I'M A BILLIONAIRE
IN DESPAIR,
NAMED DAVE,
BADLY IN NEED OF SHAVE!
I THINK
I NEED A DRINK.
SOME HONEY...
OH DEAR, DEAR,
NOT HONEY,
BEER!
PINK

AAAAGH
I AM BEING EATEN
BY A BEAR! BUT...
I AM NOT A PEAR,
I SWEAR!
MY NAME IS BONNIE,
BONNIE BLAIR.
AND I'M AN HEIR
OF A BILLIONAIRE!

I BEEN ROUND
THE HEADS OF THE PROFOUND,
BUT MY FAVORITE SKULL
WAS ONE WHICH KNEW NO DULL—
HE WAS A FAMOUS
IGNORAMOUS.

WHEN I HAVE TO CHOOSE, I DON'T FEEL I CAN WIN. I FEEL I CAN ONLY LOSE.
BUT EITHER/OR IS BETTER THAN NEITHER/NOR.

BUT I'M NOT A BOWL, I DON'T WANT HALF, I WANT THE WHOLE!

AS HARRY POTTER GROWS FAT,
AND FATTER,
GINNY WEASLEY STIRS UNEASILY.
"IS IT MY STEW
THAT MAKES HIM SO STOUT,
OR IS IT MY TROUT?"
SHE THINKS.
"OR IS IT A JINX?"

Potter, Harriet.
Proletariat.

From:
WHO?
Persons Unknown,
Briefly Shown

IF WE COUNT
FROM 10 TO 0,
HELPLESSLY HOPING
FOR THE COMING OF A HERO,
WILL HE, OR SHE, APPEAR?
3...2...1...OH, DEAR!

EVEN HIS CAR'S GOT A SCAR.
POTTER

RECIPE IDEA

SIMMER A SWIMMER
IN STRAWBERRY SEA,
SPICE WITH SANDY DEBRIS,
LET SIT IN THE SUN
UNTIL YOU'RE DONE
HAVING FUN.

IT AIN'T A SIN
TO DIG IN,
RECIPE IDEA

A LIGHT SNACK—
PUFF-PUFF HUFF,
PUFFED AND STUFFED
IN A BURLAP SACK
WRAP

"YA GOTTA SWEET DEAL,"
SAYS BANANA PEEL
TO THE DAPPER CANDY WRAPPER.
"I AM SO JEALOUS
OF ALL YA PLASTIC FELLAS!"

THE THING WAS AS BIG
AS A PRIZE-WINNING PIG!
AND THEN IT SPOKE—
"RELEASE ME, YA BLOKE,
AN I'LL GRANT YE A WISH."
SO I SAYS, "YES, MA'AM."
...AND HERE I AM!

"WE'RE IN HELL!"
CRIES HER BRAIN CELL.

"I GOT THE MOST,"
HE USED TO BOAST
TO THE BOY WITH LESS,
WHO FINALLY DID CONFESS,

HIM AND HER AND LAUGHTER,
FOREVER AFTER,

"I HOPE," SAYS SOAP,
"BUT ALL TOO SOON, I FEAR,
I SHALL DISAPPEAR."

SWIMMING
IS TRIMMING.

"BUT NOT ALL SUCCESSES
ARE YESES,"
SAYS STORMY GUESSES.

DO NOT LET YOUR SORROW
LAST PAST TOMORROW.
ENJOY IT TODAY,
THEN THROW IT AWAY.

"CAN 2 FALSES = TRUTH?"
WONDERS SEQUEL RUTH.

QUEENS

"CUT HER IN TWO!"
CRIES THE QUEEN OF BLUE.

"TOSS HER IN THE RAVINE!"
CRIES THE QUEEN OF GREEN..

"GIVE HER THE SMACK!"
CRIES THE QUEEN OF BLACK.

"THAT'S RIGHT! QUITE!"
CRIES THE QUEEN OF WHITE.

"LET'S ALL JUST CALM DOWN,"
BEGS THE QUEEN OF BROWN.

"LET'S NOT B-B-BELLOW,
LET'S BE M-M-MELLOW,"
SINGS THE QUEEN OF YELLOW.

"I AGREE, WHY DON'T WE
SMOKE HER?"
SUGGESTS THE QUEEN OF OCHRE.

"BUT," SCREAMS RED,
"HER HEAD..."

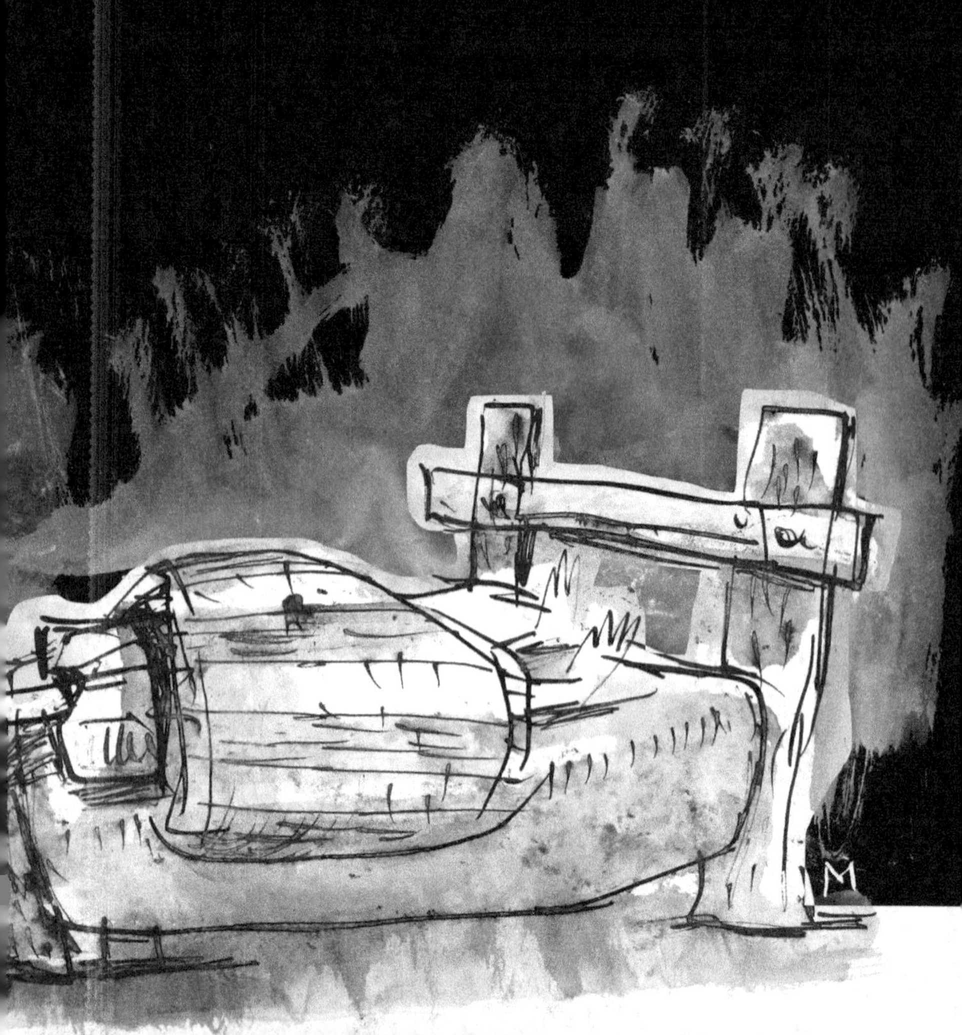

"IS TOO BIG FOR HER BED!"

"WHY DON'T SHE JUST SHRINK?"
WONDERS THE QUEEN OF PINK.
END

VIC-C-CARIOUS D-DARIUS—
HE ONLY DARE TO STARE.

A HIM
IS JUST A WHIM
WITH A MISSING LIMB.

EUGENE,
THE QUEEN OF MEAN,
CAN MAKE ANY GAL, OR GUY,
RUN HOME AND CRY.

THREE HEARTY CHEERS
FOR THY SPARKLING
TEARS!
I TAKE GREAT PLEASURE
COLLECTING YOUR
TREASURE.

ON HS HIS WAY TO HELL,
HE TRIPPED AND FELL.

OUCH!
CAN SOMEONE
TAKE ME
TO A COUCH?

DON'T POUT
SAUERKRAUT

SoSoSour
SUNFLOWER

RECIPE IDEA

TAKE A DULL PAGE
(PREFERABLY OLD
IN AGE.)

WRINKLE,

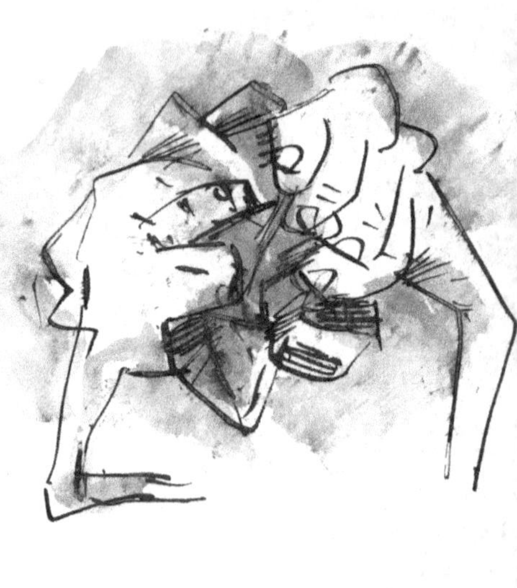

THEN SPRINKLE.
(I.E. GET IT WET)

THEN FOLD IT ONCE.

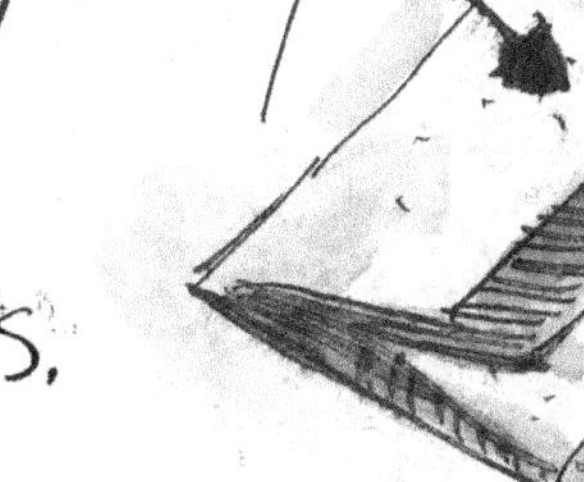
FOLD IT TWICE.

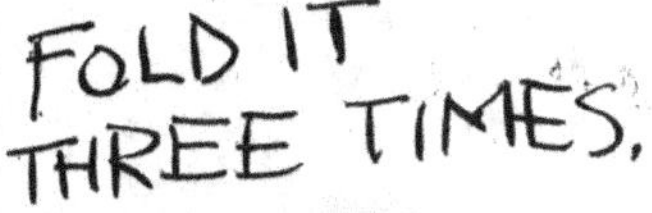
FOLD IT
THREE TIMES.

SO THAT IT
NOW RHYMES!

THIRST
FOR THE FIRST.
GENIUS JUICE
OXYMORONIC TONIC
THIRST
FOR THE WORST.

GHOST, LOST,
ON MODERN LIGHT POST,
LIGHTLY HARASSED,
PINES FOR HIS PAST.

UNDERNEATH THE PAINT,
PHONY TONY AIN'T.

RECIPE IDEA

MUMBO GUMBO

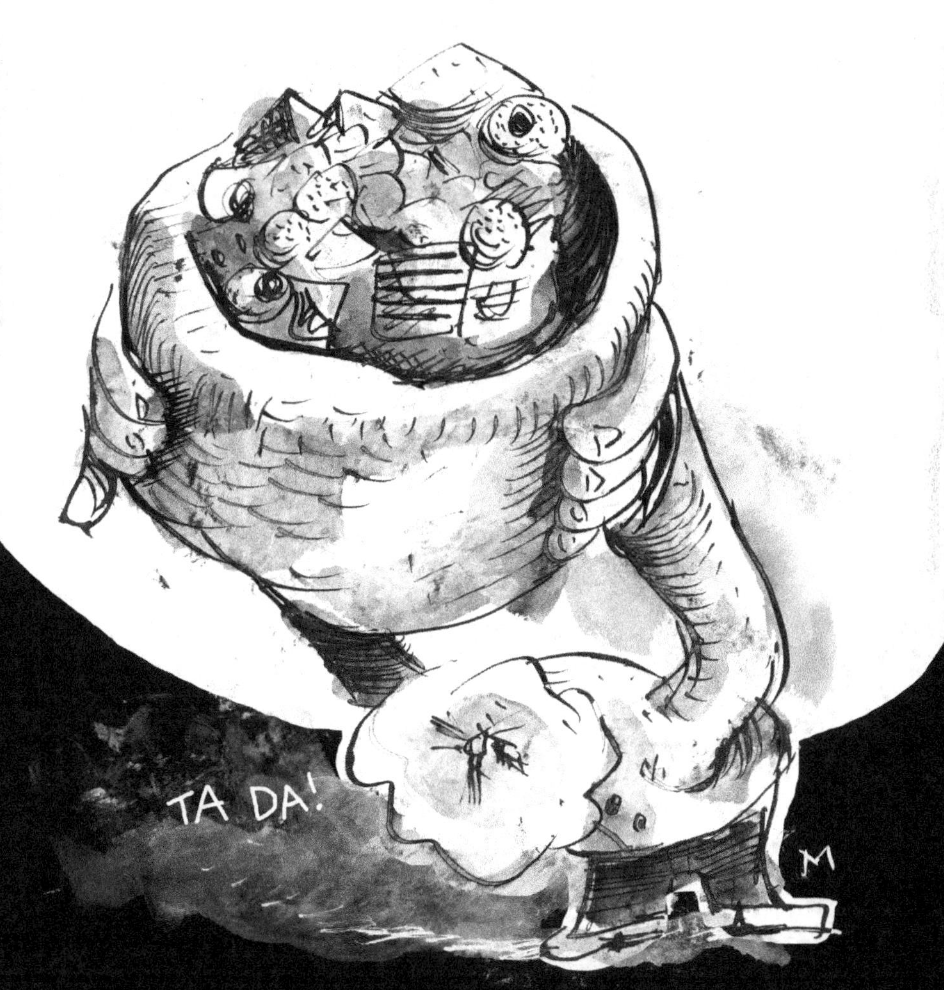

THERE AIN'T NO SMART WITHOUT ART!

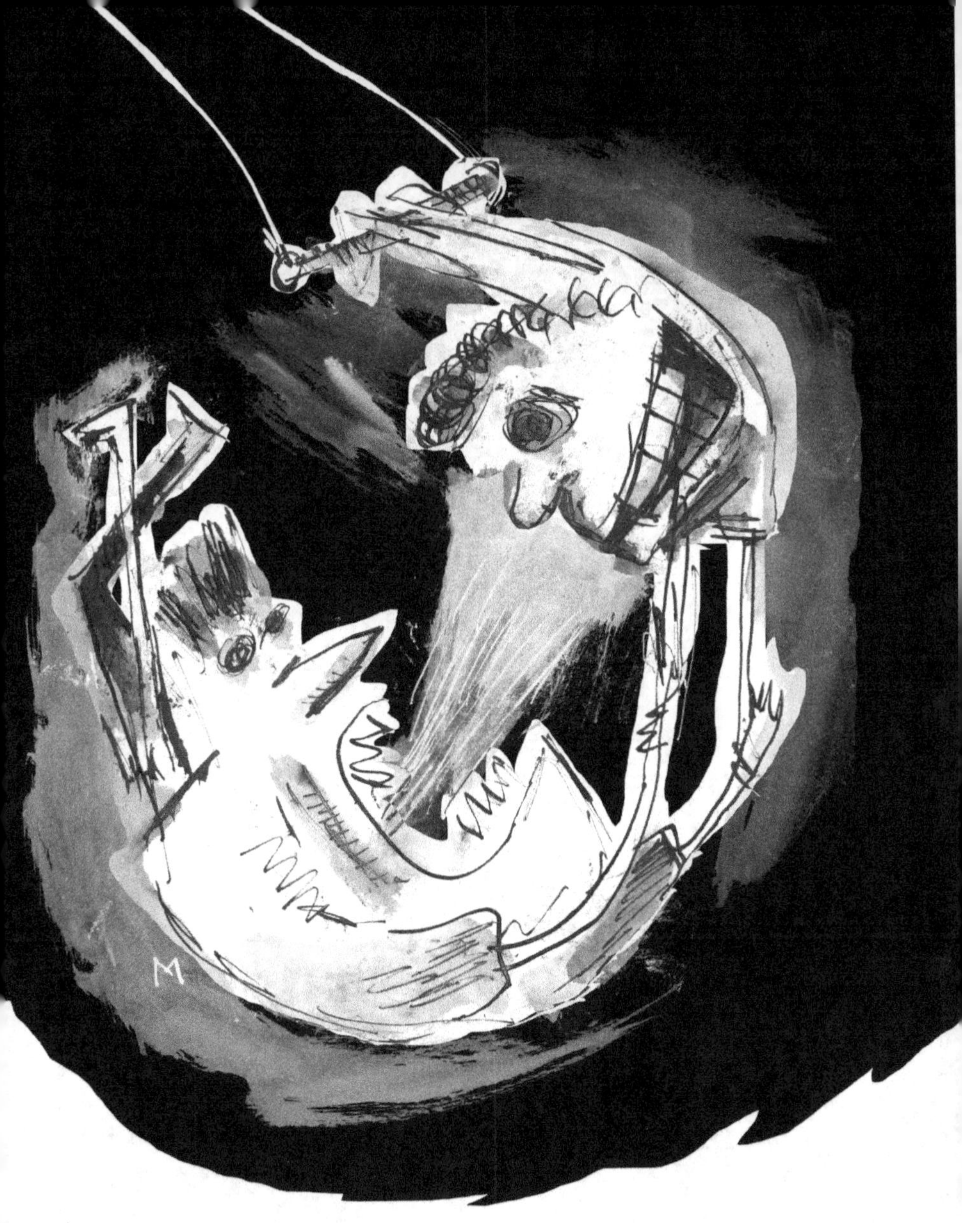

ACROBAT BRATS, SWING
FROM A STRING, SCREAMING.
AM I DREAMING?

WE WOULD PREVENT RUBBLE
IF WE COULD TRAP TROUBLE
INSIDE A THOUGHT BUBBLE.

"DO I MUTTER?"
MUSES CLUTTER.

"LET US NOW
TAKE A BRIEF BREAK,"
SAYS STOMACH ACHE.

THEY SAY THAT I'M HYPER,
BUT I DON'T NEED NO DIAPER.

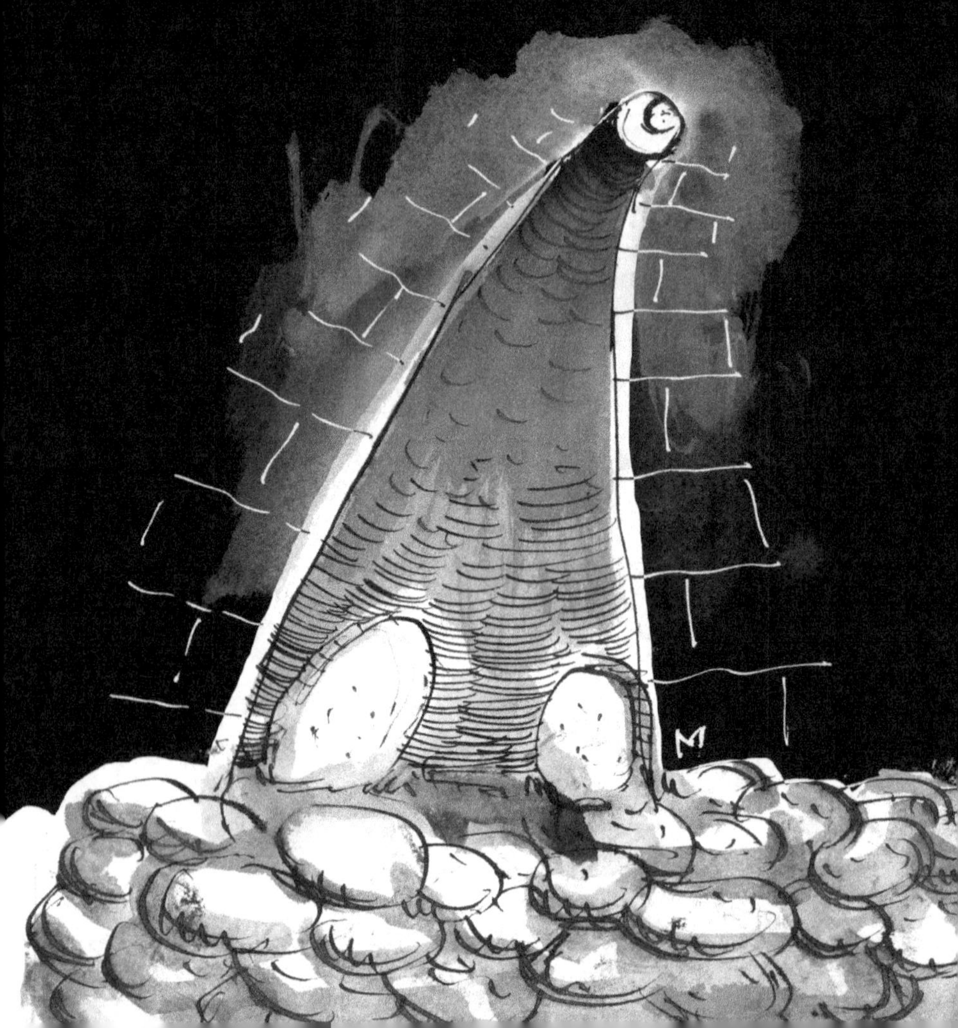

"I WISH I HADN'T FELL
INTO THE WISHING WELL,"
SAYS CENT, IN LAMENT.
"STOP YAR WISHIN'
AND CLIMB,"
SAYS THE OLD DIME.

BEFALLEN FABLE, UNABLE

ONCE— "YOU DUNCE!"
—A TALENTED ZEBRA
TALKED SMACK
TO A LION.

"DON'T YOU JUST LOVE DIRT!"
WITH TROUSERS FLIRTS A SKIRT.
WILL SHE END UP GETTING HURT?

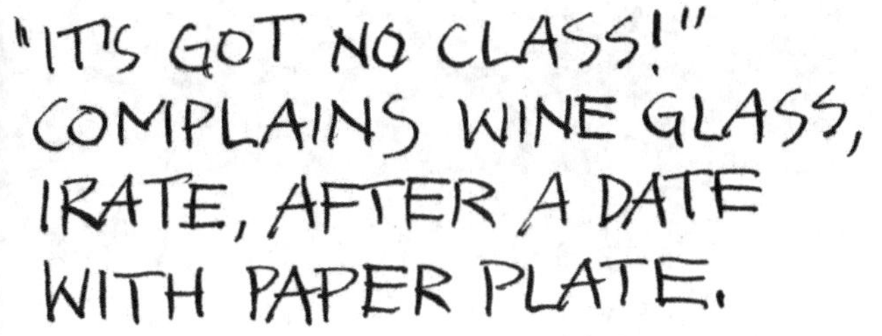

"IT'S GOT NO CLASS!"
COMPLAINS WINE GLASS,
IRATE, AFTER A DATE
WITH PAPER PLATE.

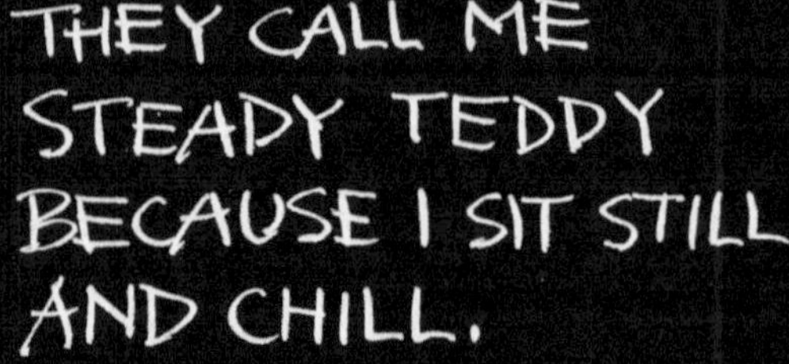
THEY CALL ME
STEADY TEDDY
BECAUSE I SIT STILL
AND CHILL.

NIGHT NEVER SLEEPS, SHE WEEPS
FOR DAY, WHO'S GONE AWAY,
LOOKING...

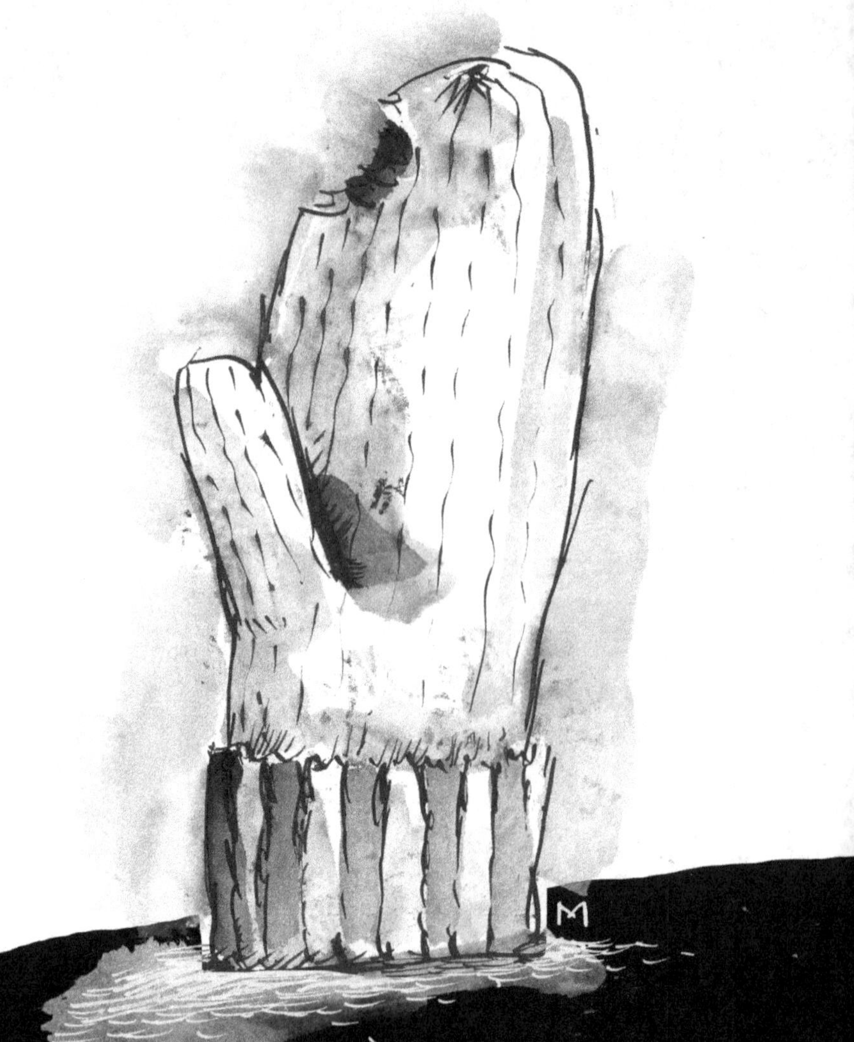

IN BRITAIN, I WAS BITTEN
BY A BOY NAMED CORY.
WANNA HEAR THE STORY?

"HER FACE
WAS A DISGRACE!"

"CLOSE YOUR EYES
AND PRETEND THAT YOU'RE PRETTY,"
SAYS MORTICIAN BEAUTICIAN
WITH SYMPATHY AND PITY.
"NOW OPEN THEM. [A SMIRK]
NOPE, IT DIDN'T WORK."

COULD WE BE SINKING
FROM TOO MUCH
THINKING?

"THAT ARMY BOOT IS A BRUTE!"
SQUEAKS THE DAINTY BLACK STILETTO.
"HE'S ALL GHETTO!"
BUT TEN MONTHS LATER
THEY HAVE TWINS—
CUTE LITTLE BABY MOCCASINS.

"I DO I DO I DO I DO!" SAYS MY SHOE.
"I WILL FOREVER YOU CHERISH,
UNTIL YOU PERISH."

"MOTHER, I WANNA LIVE IN A BUBBLE,
IF THAT AIN'T TOO MUCH TROUBLE."

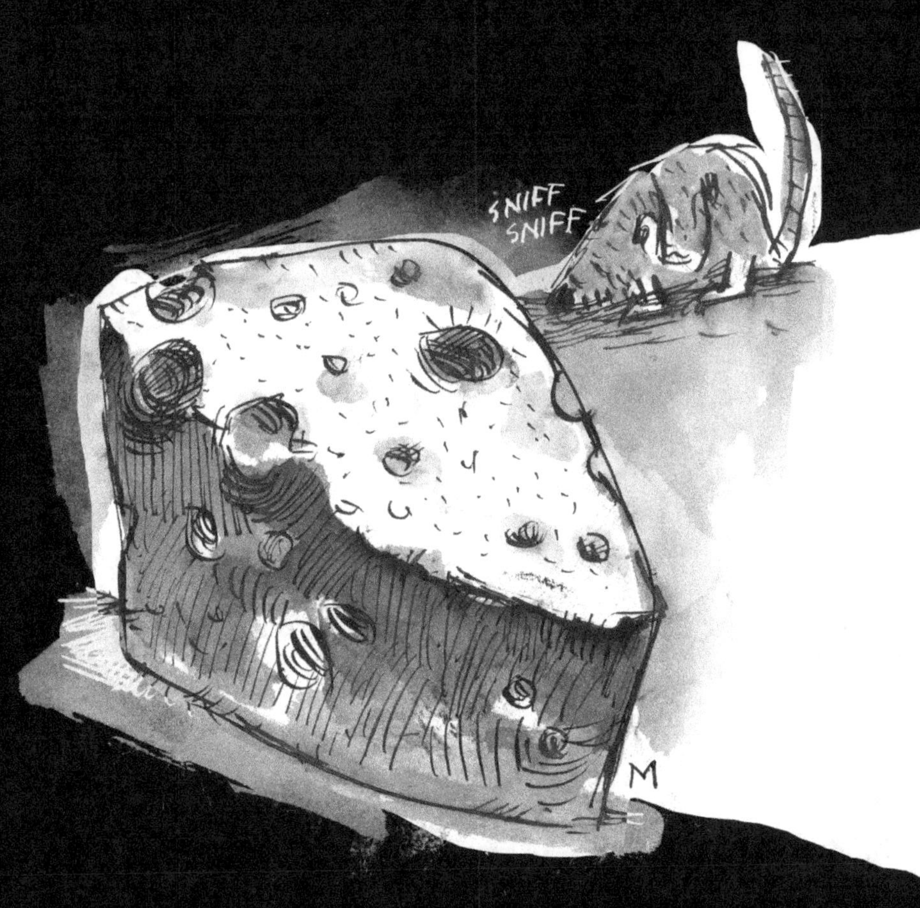

"I MAY BE OLD,
BUT I'M AS BEAUTIFUL AS GOLD,"
TO MOLD SAYS CHEESE,
WHO THINKS, "OH, PLEASE!"
BUT SMILES, AND SAYS
"I AGREES, I AGREES."
SNIFF SNIFF

IF YOU GOTTA CROWN,
YOU MAY SIT DOWN.
IF NOT,
YOU GOTTA SQUAT.

JOE IS IN THE SLAMMER
FOR USING BAD GRAMMAR.
"I SWEAR I DID NOT KNOW
T'WERE 'GAINST THE LAW, MA!"

RRRRRIP
LOVE, TORN ASUNDER...
DRIP
KINDA MAKES YA WONDER...
DRIP
HMM... NO, NOT REALLY...
DRIP
IT'S PROBABLY SOMETHING SILLY...
PLOP
JUST GRAB A BUCKET
AND A MOP.

A PILLOW WET FROM TEARS
SNEERS—
"GO TAKE A SHOWER
AND WASH OFF YOUR DOUR!
OR JUMP IN THE POOL,
YOU SILLY, YOUNG FOOL."

THAT FELLA
LOVES HIS UMBRELLA
MORE THAN THAT FELLA
LOVES STELLA.
"I THINK MY UMBRELLA
HAS MORE USES," HE MUSES.
THAT IS A BAD FELLA.
YOU OUGHT TO LEAVE HIM, STELLA.
AND TAKE HIS UGLY UMBRELLA!

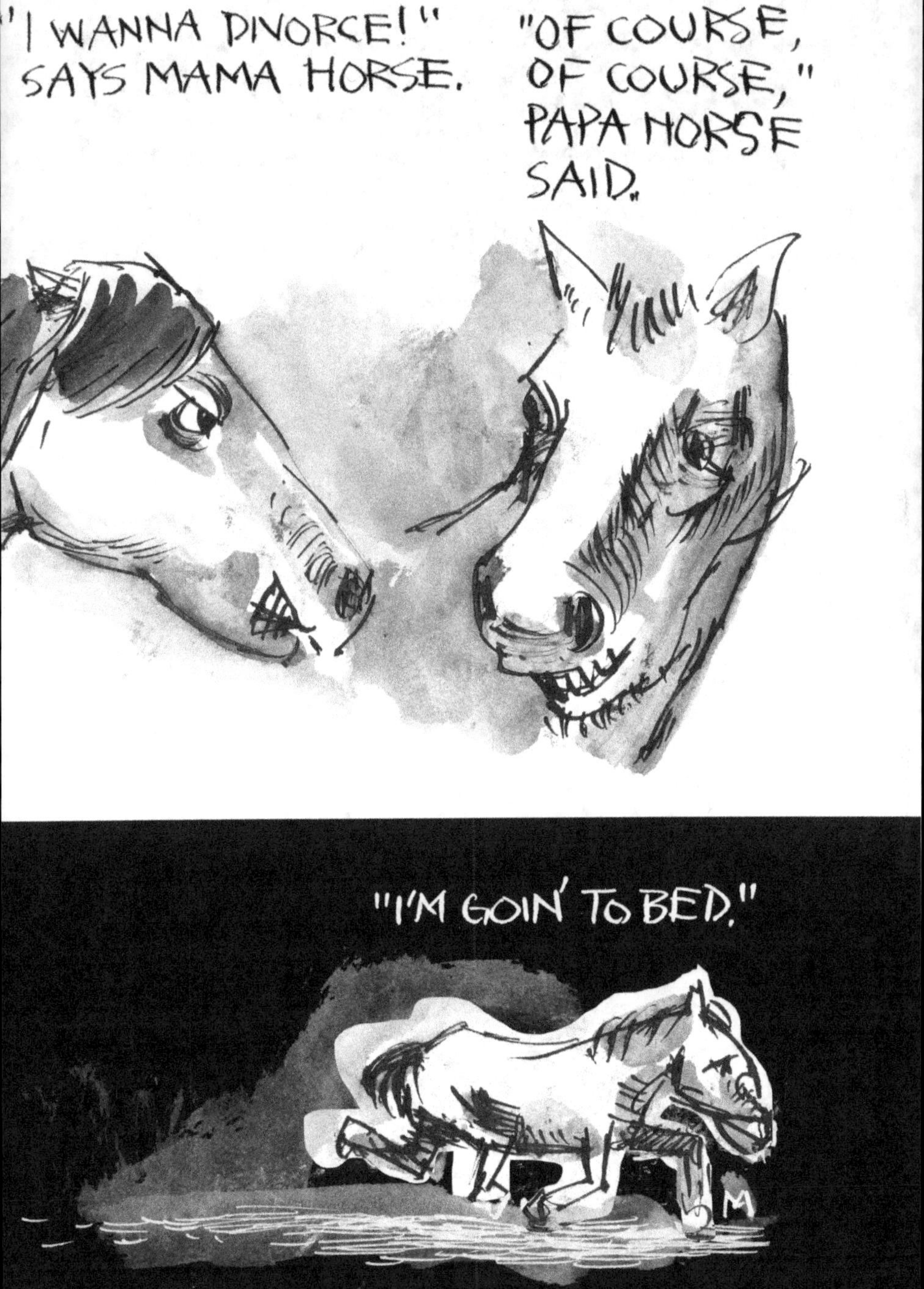

"I WANNA DIVORCE!"
SAYS MAMA HORSE.
"OF COURSE,
OF COURSE,"
PAPA HORSE
SAID.

"I'M GOIN' TO BED."

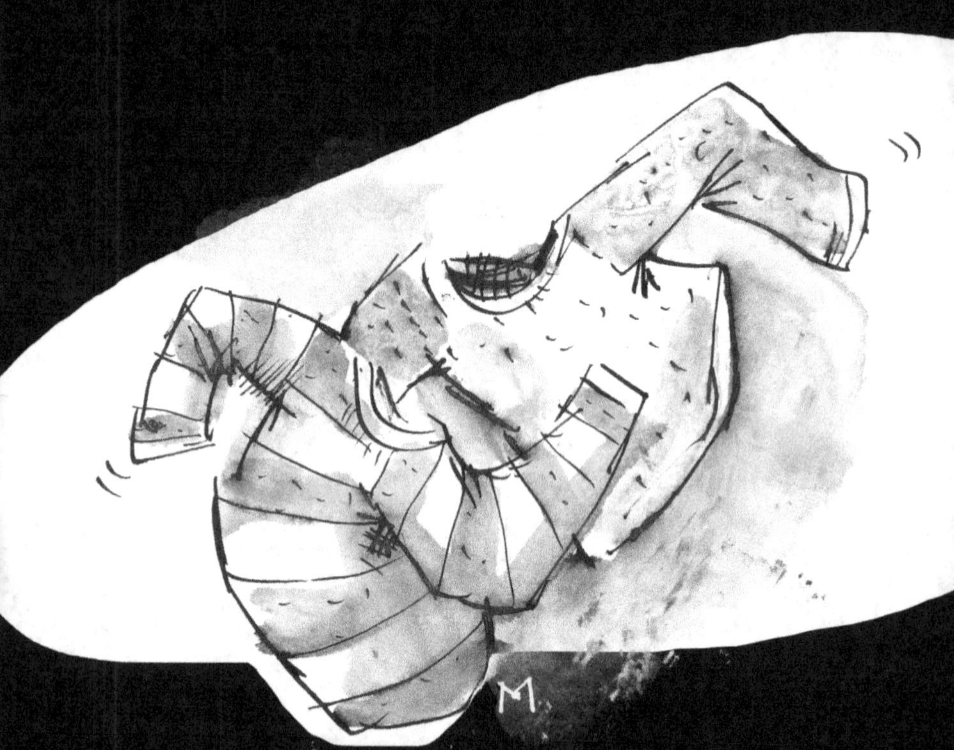

THERE IS A KERFUFFLE
INSIDE MY DUFFEL—
MY TWO SHIRTS DISAGREE
WHICH IS THE ONE
THAT LOOKS BEST ON ME.

M.

BIRTHDAY BLUES

TO THE SKIRT
COMPLAINS THE SHIRT—
"WHEN SHE WAS SIZE 6,
I WAS IN HEAVEN.
BUT TODAY,
SHE TURNED SIZE 7!"

HE, HIM
A MIND DEFINED
IS A MIND CONFINED
IN A ROOM
IN A TOMB.
-M

THE MEDIOCRE MIND
CRAVES TO BE CONFINED,
SHELTERED IN A BOX
AMONG ITS KINDRED BLOCKS.

YOU AIN'T NO ACTOR,
YOU'RE A NUCLEAR REACTOR!
1

AND YOU AIN'T NO DIRECTOR,
YOU'RE A HACK
AND A
HECTOR!!!...

FILMING
OF "THE LANGUID LOTUS"
HAS BEEN CANCELLED
UNTIL FURTHER NOTICE.
—PRODUCERS

"BEING WISE IS A BORE,"
ADMITS DUMBLEDORE.
"FROM NOW ON,
I SHALL ONLY PREACH
FROM SOME MERRY
MEDITERRANEAN BEACH."

"I AM CHIEF," SAYS BEEF.
"YOU ARE DORK," SAYS PORK.

"YOU ARE UNDER ARREST
  FOR FAILING THE TEST."
"BUT... BUT... I DID MY BEST!"
  TO THE JUDGE CRIES SYLVESTER.
"THEN YOU SHOULD HAVE
  DONE BESTER.
  CASE CLOSED.
  JAIL.
  FOR ONE SEMESTER."

I HONEST(WINK,WINK)LY THINK...

I HEAR A MASTER LIAR
SING IN A CHURCH CHOIR—
EACH OF HIS NOTES
ARE LOVELY MISQUOTES.

"IT'LL BE A CINCH,"
SAYS THE INCH TO THE FOOT.
"TO GET THE LOOT—
WE GO IN, WE SHOUT,
THEN WE GO OUT,"
"THAT SEEMS HARD,"
COMPLAINS THE YARD,
WHILE THE MILE
CAN ONLY SMILE.

I FIGHT.
I CHOOSE.
I MIGHT...
I MIGHT...
I LOSE.

RECIPE IDEA

SAUTÉED STEEL PIE
BOIL
A METAL COIL
IN 10W-40 MOTOR OIL.
MAKE CRUST OUT OF RUST.

UNWANTED THOUGHT, FRAUGHT—
UNINVITED GUEST, A PEST
IN THE ATTIC, TOXIC, STATIC.

"I CAN STOP AN HOUR,"
SAYS THE GIRL WITH TIME POWER.
"SO WHAT? I CAN, TOO,
MAYBE MORE."
"NA-AA. NO, YOU CAN'T!"
"YES, I CAN!
I'VE DONE IT BEFORE
WITHOUT GETTING SORE,"
SAYS HALF-DEAF STEPH,

THEN, STOUT, RUNS OUT
AND STOMPS ON TWO FLOWERS
FOR TWO AND A HALF HOURS.

AR' YA LIL' FELLA MAD?!
YA MUST O' SWALLOWED
A GALLON O' PAINT
'CAUSE I SHORE AINT!
HELLO,
ARE YOU
ME DAD?

"BETTER BICEPS,
BETTER BRAINS,"
HE TO HER
HUMANLY MANSPLAINS.

A COOK, MISTOOK
FOR A SMALL TIME CROOK,
SITS IN JAIL,
TURNING STALE.

THERE IS A TALL-TALE IN JAIL
REFUSING TO TALK
UNTIL IT'S ALLOWED TO WALK
FREE—"I WANNA GUARANTEE,
IN WRITIN', PROP'RLY SIGNED!
ONLY DEN
WILL I UNLOCK MA MIND."

A PIG GETS WINGS FROM A BAT,
STRAPS ON A PILOT'S HAT,
UNCURLS HER TINY TAIL,
AND, PAIL, STEPS TO THE EDGE
AND MAKES A PLEDGE—
"I PLEDGE
I SHALL FLY OFF THIS LEDGE...

...ONE DAY,
BUT NOT TODAY."
—AND RUNS AWAY.

"WHY DONCHA SELL YAR STUPID TA CUPID!" TO JOHNNY SAYS CONNIE, THEN BAILS TO SHARPEN HER NAILS.

WHO ARE YOU?
AND WHAT
ARE YOU DOING
STANDING
ON MY CEILING?.

YOU OUGHT TO BE KNEELING!

MARY HAD A LITTLE LAMB.
SHE NAMED HER SAM.
THEN SHE HAD ANOTHER—
PAM, SAM'S BABY BROTHER.

I'LL NEED
AT LEAST A DOZEN
TO BEAT MY COUSIN.

"DAMN THAT LITTLE LAMB!"
SAYS MARY, IN A HURRY,
"TO SUCCEED, I NEED
A DODGE RAM."

"I DON'T CARE
'BOUT NO STRUGGLE.
I JUST WANNA SNUGGLE,"
HER BOYFRIEND MAGICIAN
TELLS MAGGIE THE MUGGLE.

MAGGIE,
DON'T BE CRAGGY.
BEIN' HEROIC
IS SOOO
MESOZOIC!

YOU DON'T NEED
NO MAGIC WAND
TO MAKE BRUNETTE
A BLONDE.

HER BLACK SHOES
HAVE GOT THE BLUES
BECAUSE THEM OLD PAIR,
SHE NO LONGER WEAR.

"THAT KNIFE
THREATENS MY LIFE!"
CRIES CAKE, CUT IN HALF,
AS PARTYGOERS SING AND LAUGH.

IN NEW ORLEANS,
SHE ATE BAD BEANS.

IN NEW YORK,
SHE ATE BAD PORK.

AHH, THEM YESTER-YEARS, WHEN I COULD DROWN A WHOLE TOWN...
THIS DARK GRAY CLOUD
SMILES MUCH, MUCH TOO LOUD.
WHY DOES IT LOOK
SO FILLED WITH BLISS?
BECAUSE IT LOVES TO REMINISCE
ABOUT THE AGE OF YORE
WHEN IT WOULD SOAR, SOAR,
AND THUNDER AND ROAR.

NIMBOSTRATUS ON APPARATUS
GETS THINNER FOR DINNER
BY SHEDDING SOME SNOW
ON THE PLATEAU BELOW.

A NIMBLE
CUMULONIMBUS
HIP-HOPS IN THE SKY
KEEPING DRY.

"HOW LONG
DOES YOU PRACTICE
AT BEING A CACTUS?"

"WHAT SILLY DRIVEL!"
SAYS BRUTE OF CIVIL.

THE TIGRESS CROUCHES
ON LIVING ROOM COUCHES,
AND SPRINGS
AT UNSUSPECTING LIVING THINGS.
"COLOR ME BEFUDDLE,
BUT, I THINK," SAYS THE SHRINK,
"SHE JUST WANTS TO CUDDLE."

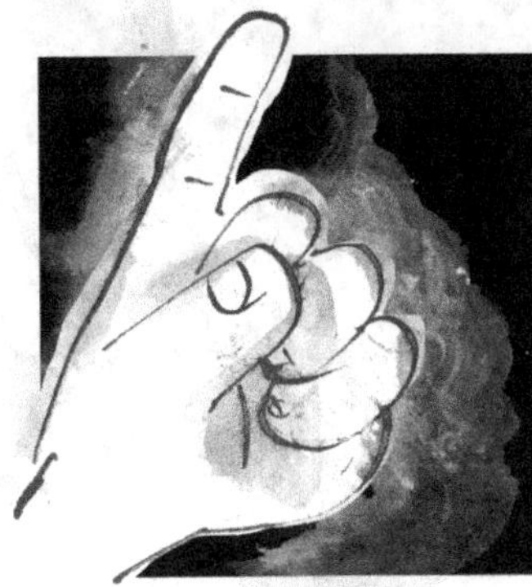

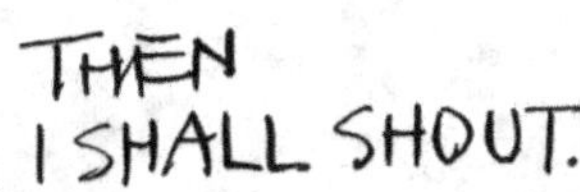
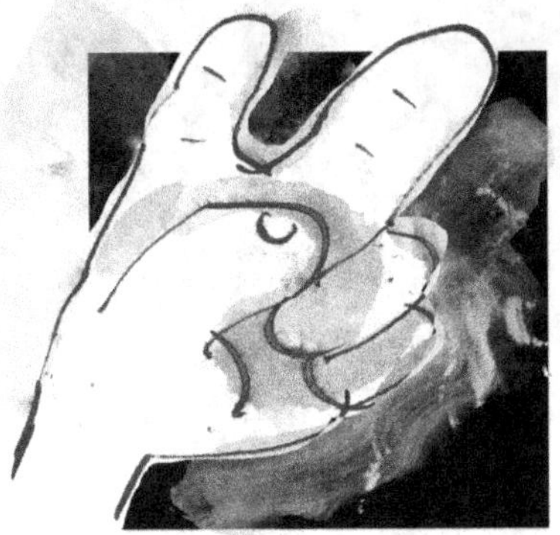

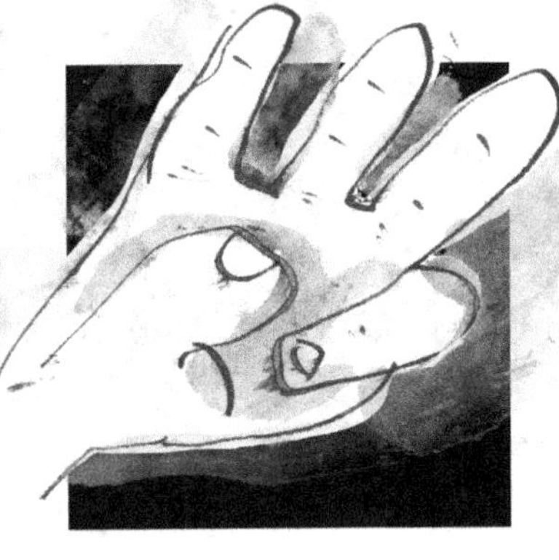

PLEASE ASK ME WHY!

HER TWO BIG TOES
PUT ON AIRS,
BUT NO ONE CARES.
"BOW BEFORE US,"
THEY COMMAND
ONLY TO BE TICKLED
BY A FRIVOLOUS FOREIGN
HAND.

WE ARE TOO
PROFOUND...
1

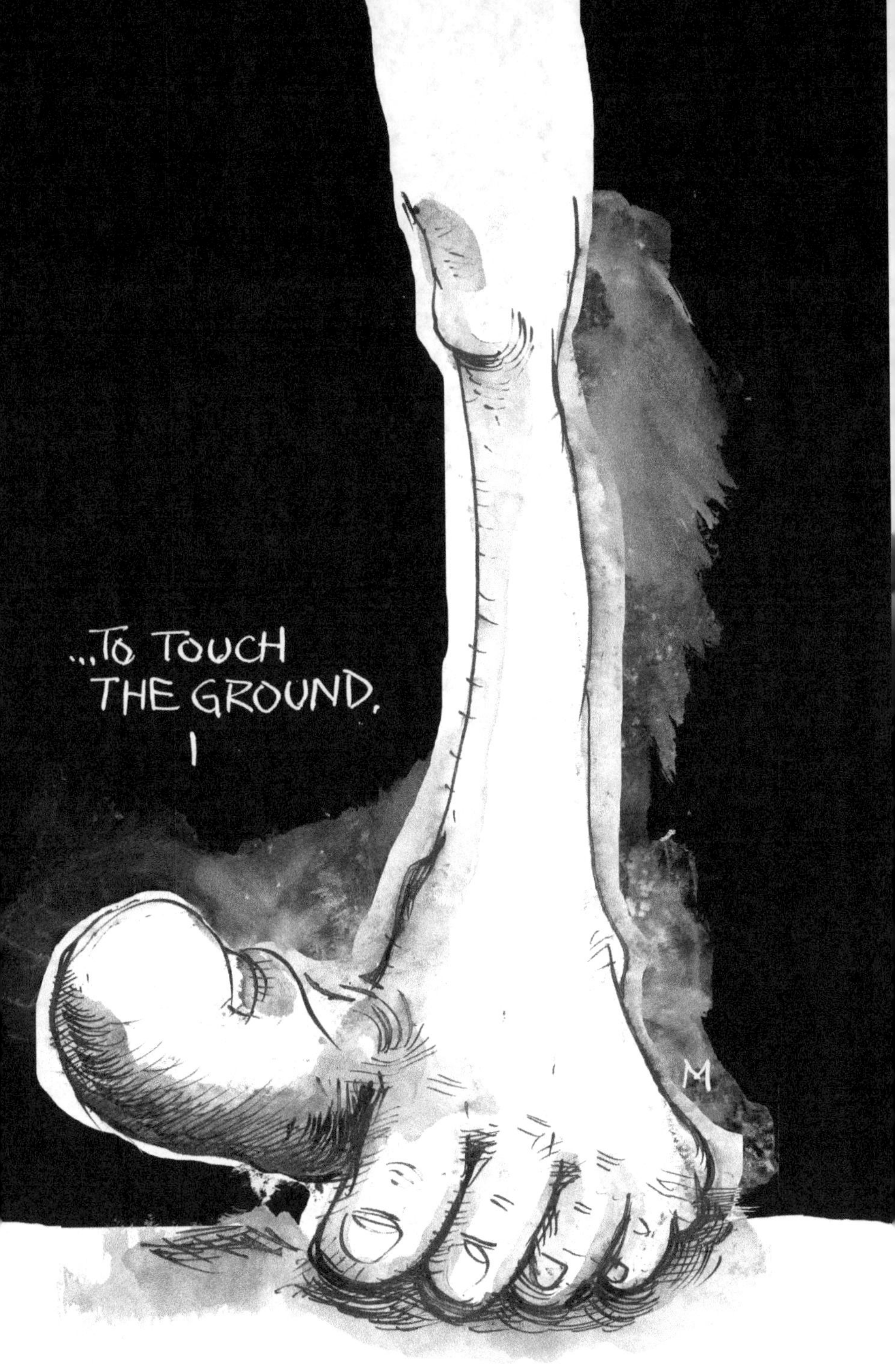
...TO TOUCH
THE GROUND.

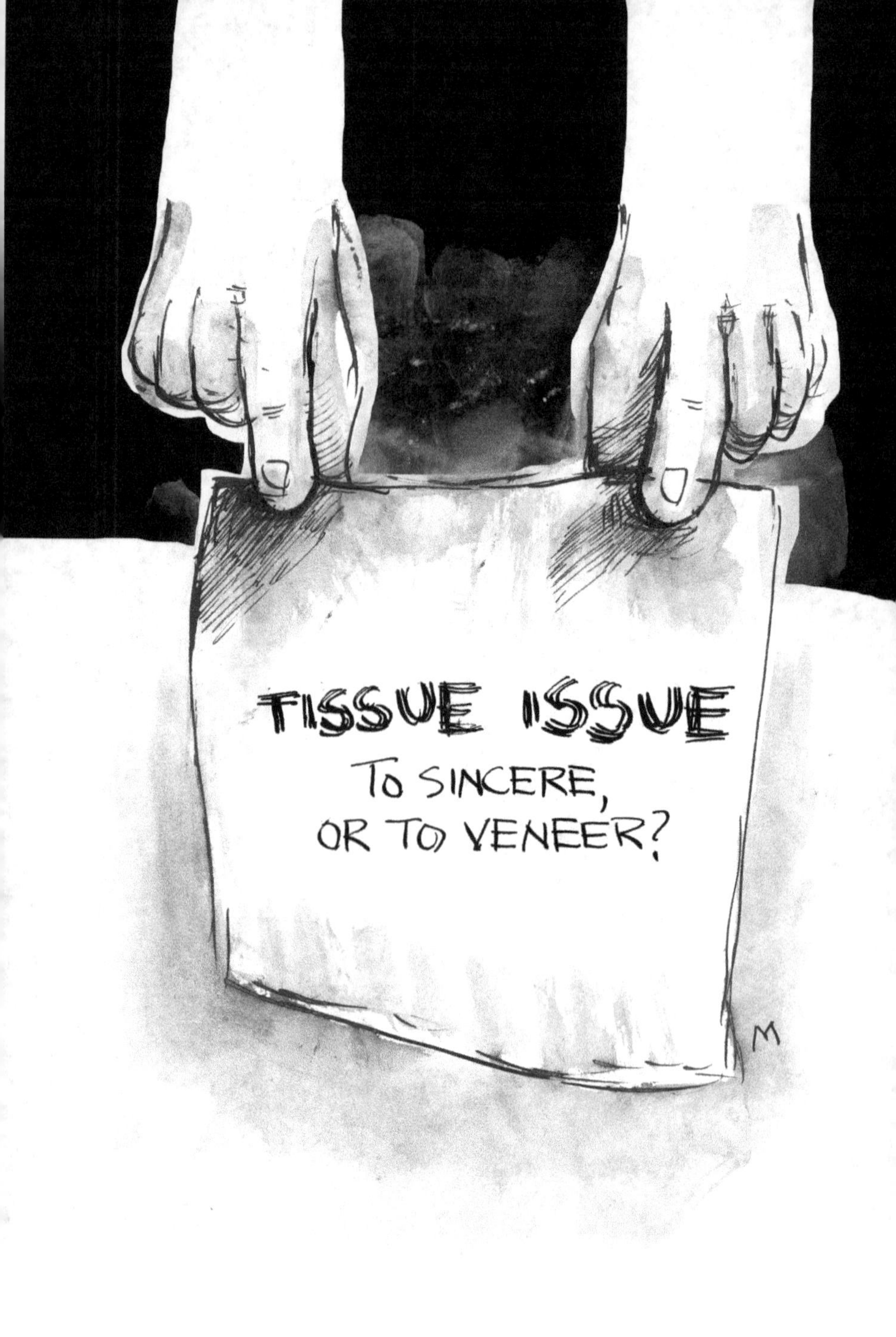

TISSUE ISSUE
TO SINCERE,
OR TO VENEER?

THOU SHALT NOT HAVE MORE THAN THY NEIGHBORE!

COMMANDS A VOICE, DOUR, FROM ATOP AN IVORY TOWER.

TU CASA ES MI CASA.

TWO ROWS OF TOES
I CAN'T STOP MYSELF
FROM KISSING.
"OUCH!
LOOK WHAT YA DONE, HON,
ONE O' MY TOES
IS NOW MISSIN'!"

RECIPE IDEA

POTATOE SOUP

BOIL A DIGIT
OF A PLUMP MIDGET,
ADD 10 PLEAS,
AND 1 LB. OF CHEESE.

FOR SEVEN DAYS
AND SEVEN NIGHTS,
IT'S BEEN RAINING
AMOOLAMOO KNIGHTS.
OUT OF THE SKY THEY FALL,
CRASH TO THE GROUND,
PICK THEMSELVES UP,
AND BEGIN TO BRAWL!

"WHAT IS LIFE,"
THE KNIGHTS LAMENT,
"BUT A GLORIOUS TOURNAMENT!
LIFE WITHOUT VIOLENCE
AND GORE,
WE SIR KNIGHTS
ALL DEPLORE."

SHE TWEETED
OVERHEATED,
AND NOW REGRETS
HER EMPTY THREATS.

NOW KNOWETH HER TRUE FRIENDS
PARIAH MARIAH PROFOUNDLY
STANDS.

THOUGH KRISTINE
BE ONLY A QUEEN,
HER FACE
IS AN ACE!

TAKE A SEAT
AND EAT,
BUT NOT THE SEAT!

MISTER THRILL
SITS ON A SILL,
WO-WO-WOBBLES,
AND BLOWS BLISSFUL BUBBLES
AT PASSING-BY TROUBLES.

HOPE
ON TIGHTROPE
TIPTOES...
FLY FLAPS ITS WINGS..
WIND BLOWS...

A SWARM OF BEES
RELEASE A BREEZE
OF BUZZWORDS
IN BURMESE.

"EXPLAIN THIS CHEESE,
PLEASE."

SHE
WANTS TO BE HE,
SO SHE DELETES HER S
AND BECOMES LES.

LUCIFER (SHE, HER)

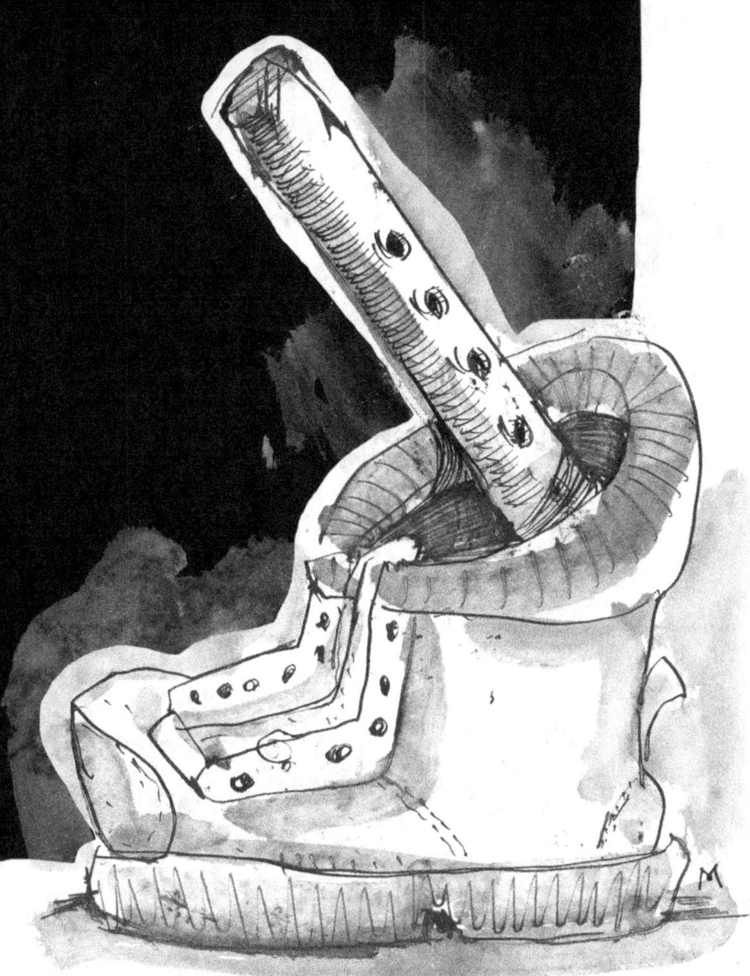

THE FLUTE
SCORNS THE BOOT.

A BITTER BEE BIT A BUTT.
TUT! TUT!
SHE OUGHT BETTER BITTED
BROTHER BERNIE'S
BIG HEAD, INSTEAD.

SHE IS SUSPICIOUS
OF ANY DELICIOUS—
"WHY WOULD
IT TASTE SO GOOD?"

THE PRISM OF PESSIMISM

AN IMPLEMENT OF OPPRESSION, FORGED FROM THE SINISTER DARK DIAMOND BY THE SEVEN DEADLY SAINTS, THE PRISM IS A DIM TOOL OF POWER FULL BULL.

WITH THIS WRETCHED RELIC, THE DEEPLY DEPLORED DARK LORD ENLISTS HIS DOUR ARMY OF PESSIMISTS AND ENTHRALLS WITHIN ITS CRACKED CRYSTAL WALLS.

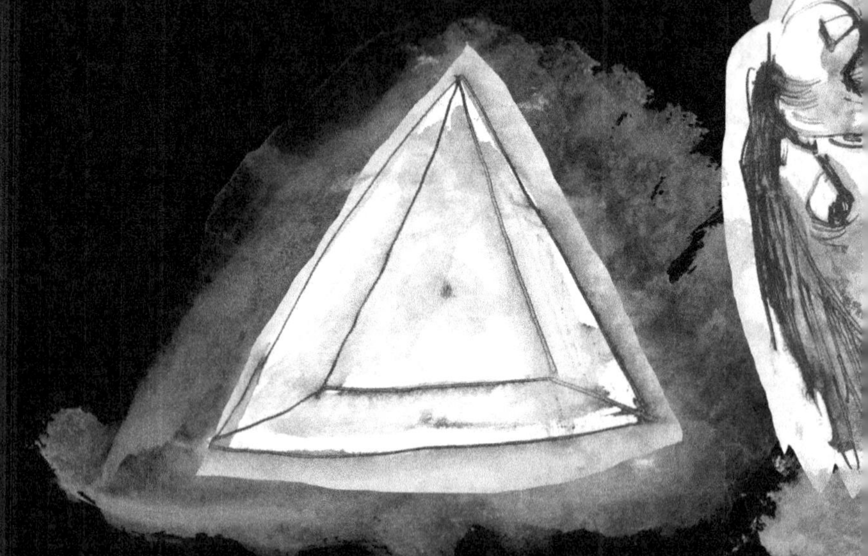

UNDER ITS SULLEN SPELL, IN MISERY
MILLIONS OF DENIZENS DWELL,
STRESSED, DEPRESSED AND
OBSESSED.

THE P.O.P. TWISTS AND TWISTS
UNTIL ITS VICTIM'S MIND
BECOMES A PAIR OF CLENCHED
FISTS, FROM HENCE FOREVER
FILLED WITH MALEVOLENCE.

THE LITTLE SUPERHEROES
BATTLE BULL
IN SCHOOL
AND PERNICIOUS PREACHERS
DISGUISED AS TEACHERS.

FOR THESE SUPERVILLAINS WE PRESCRIBE OUR, HOMEMADE PENICILLINS.
WE SQUASH HOGWASH!

FALL IS THE SEASON
FOR THE SPRING OF REASON
BUT AMIDST PERFIDIOUS PERFUME
REASON CAN'T BLOOM,

WE LEARN TO DISCERN
AND UNPEEL
TO GET TO THE CORE
OF THE TRUE
AND THE REAL.

THE WISE
CAN SEE THROUGH DISGUISE.

LIES
DO NOT BECOME TRUTHS
JUST BECAUSE THEY'RE BELIEVED
BY BILLIONS OF YOUTHS.

RECIPE IDEA

SWEET DECEIT

RECIPE IDEA

TEACH AND SCREECH

IT'S A CRISIS!
IT'S A CRISIS!
(MOLTEN ICE IS.)

THE END IS NIGH!
THE END IS NIGH!
(PLEASE STAND BY.)

CYNIC

IN THE CLINIC FOR THE CYNIC
SITS A BIRD, DETERRED—
"I DON'T BELIEVE IN LOVE!"
BOASTS THE BITTER, DARK DOVE,
WHOSE HEART TURNED WRONG
FROM FLYING ALONE FOR TOO LONG.

LOVE
IS A HOAX
TO FOOL NAIVE
BLOKES.

ONCE BURNT,
FOREVER LEARNT.

YOU'RE PRETTY,
PITY.

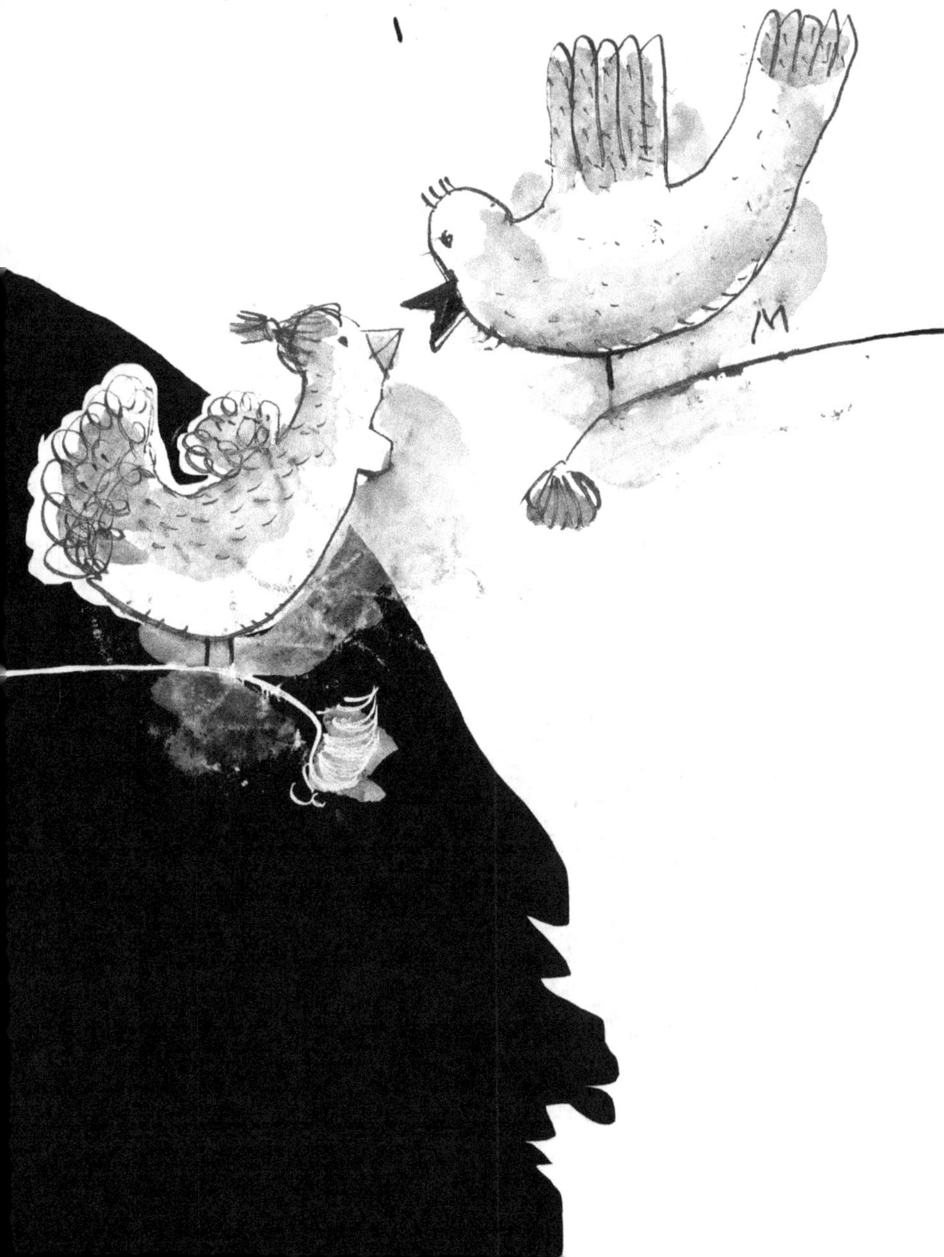

I DON'T WANT
TO BOAST,
BUT I HAVE LOVED
AND I HAVE LOST!

YESTER TIME,
I STROVE
FOR LOVE.
BUT NOW,
I ONLY STRIVE
'CAUSE I'M ALIVE.

HER POISON
STILL LINGERS,
IN MY HEART
AND ON MY
FING WINGERS.

LUV IS A TURD,
NOT FIT
FUR A BIRD.

ONE WAY
O' ANOTHER,
LUV WILL BREAK YA,
BROTHER.

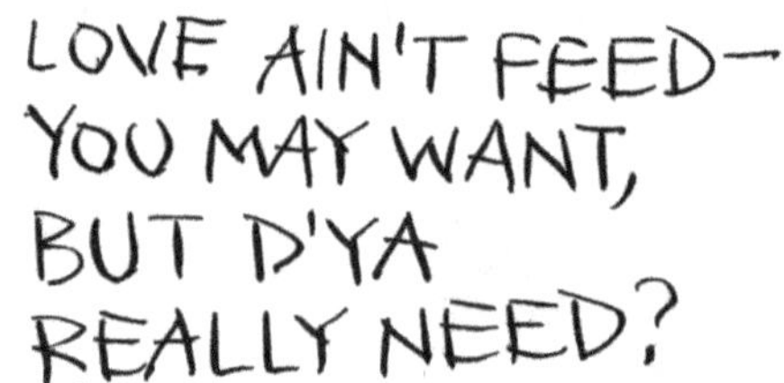

LOVE AIN'T FEED—
YOU MAY WANT,
BUT D'YA
REALLY NEED?

MY SWEET 'N' SALTY SISTER,
LUV IS A BLEATIN' BLISTER!

END

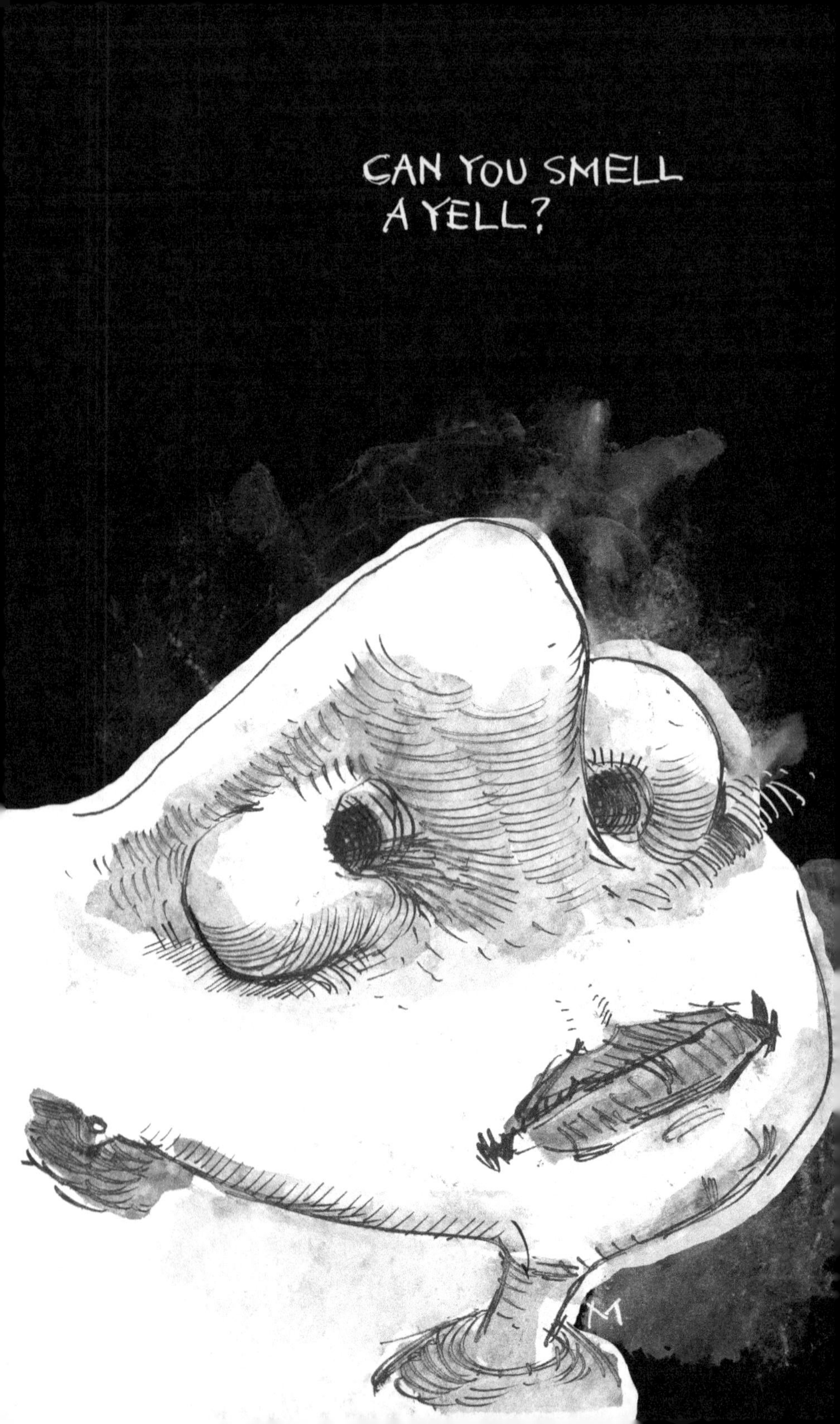

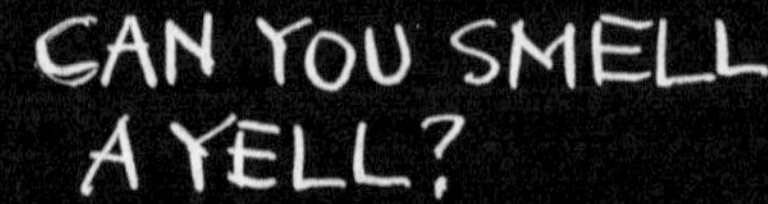

CAN YOU SMELL
A YELL?

CAN YOU HEAR
A TEAR?

CAN'T WE
JUST PRETEND
THAT WE'RE
AT THE END?

I SEE A COCKROACH
APPROACH
ON THE KITCHEN FLOOR.
THE LITTLE PEST
HAS ZEST.
HE SAYS, "HELLO, JOE.
I'M SO HUNGRY,
I COULD EAT A BOAR!
MAYBE EVEN FOUR,
HAR HAR HAR!
WHATCHA GOT IN THE FRIDGE?
WANNA PLAY SOME BRIDGE
(YAAAWN) LATER ON?"

NOT-FOR-ELISE BETO BERNICE
HATES ALL THAT "ROMANTIC CHEESE."
SHE DOESN'T GET WEAK IN THE KNEES,
AND HER LEATHER BELT DON'T MELT,
WHEN SOFT-MELODY CODY CROONS
HIS "SLUGGISH, STUPID, MOLDY TUNES
ABOUT FOOL MOONS AND STARRY NIGHTS
AND HEROIC WHITE KNIGHTS
IN THEIR BLOODY SHINING ARMOUR!"

SWINE
MAY NOT SO SHINE,
BUT THEY'RE NO LESS
DIVINE.

SHE IS HAPP'LY MARRIED
TO FRANK THE FARMER.

I LOVE
MY STABLE STUD
ENCRUSTED IN
SWEAT AND MUD.
SMELLING OF CATTLE,
NOT BATTLE.

"HOW ARE YOU DOING THIS, MISS?
ARE YOU A WITCH?" ASKS THE SWITCH,
IN WONDER, AWAITING THUNDER.

A GOOD MORNING WARNING

SOME OF US MAY SOON BECOME
AS SOFT AS BUBBLE GUM —
OUR BODIES, BULBOUS POT;
OUR BRAINS, ROT.

LURKING
BEHIND THE VEIL OF TEARS—
LAUGHTER AND CHEERS?

AROUND THE BEND
CROUCHES THE END,
READY TO SPRING
AT EACH LIVING THING.

EPIPHANY ANNIE HAD, AND IT MADE HER MAD!

TWO POMPLY PEOPLE
ON A SLIPPERY STEEPLE STAND
AND DEMAND.

"I CONFESS!
I CONFESS!
I'M A NO,
NOT A YES!"

A CHILL ON A HILL
STEAMS AS IT DREAMS
OF A BEACH IN BRAZIL.

WILL HER TIRED MUM
SUCCOMB
TO HER TANTRUM DRUM,
OR WILL SHE JOIN IN THE BEAT
ON BETTY'S SOFT SEAT?
BEING IN THIS MUSICAL DUET,
BETTY'S BOTTOM
MAY REGRET YET.

HE HAD A MINUTE,
BUT WANTED MORE POWER,
SO HE TOOK AN HOUR.

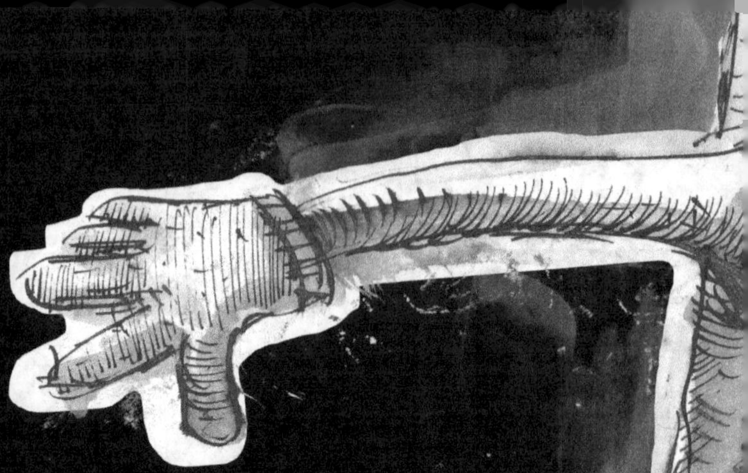

THIS TRUNK
IS IN A FUNK.
"MY CROWN IS BARE
'CAUSE I LOST ALL MY HAIR!
I FEEL SO OLD,
AND IT'S GETTING COLD."
"MAYBE WE COULD GET
A BLANKET OR WARM WIG."
SUGGESTS A SHIVERING TWIG.

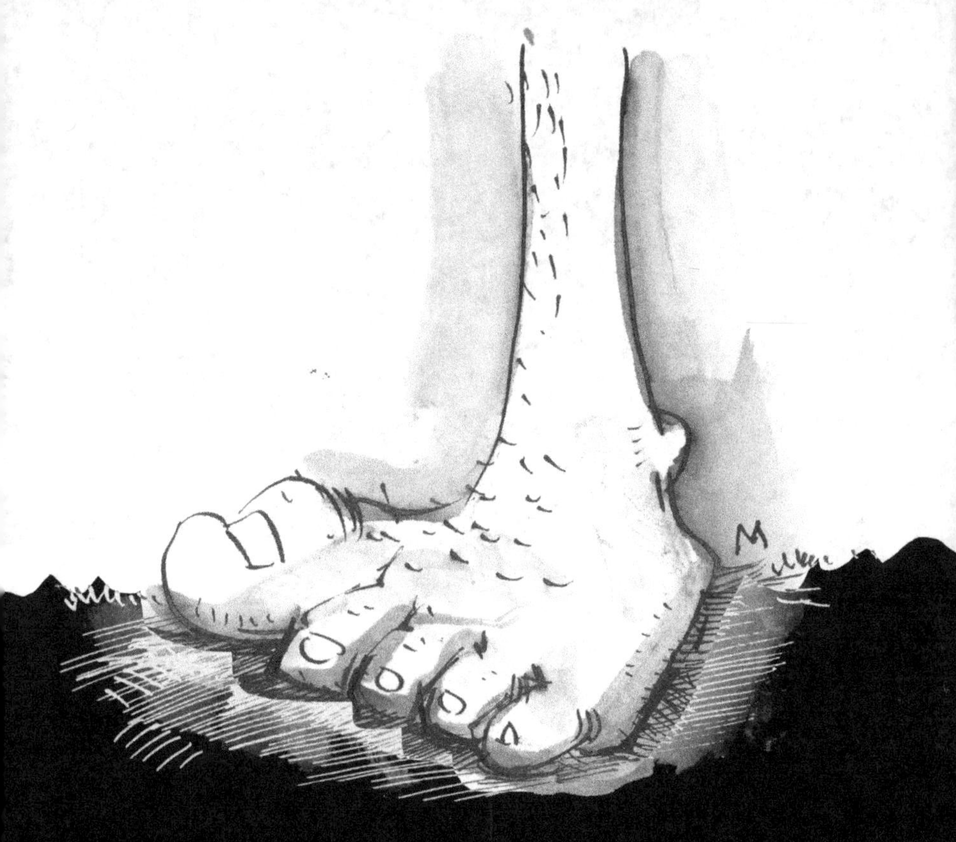

ROOTS WITHOUT BOOTS

HOW MANY TOES?
NO ONE KNOWS!
YET EACH TOE
DWELLS WITHIN ITS OWN PRIVATE WOE—
"I WANT TO BE FREE, FREE!
BUT INSTEAD,
I'M ATTACHED TO THIS TREE."

I DID, I DO, I DOES.
I IS, I WAS, I BE BECAUSE
I LOVE THE BUZZ
OF ALL APPLAUSE!

Farm + Charm = Harm

"YA CAIN'T BE CHARMIN'
WHILE YAR FARMIN'
'CAUSE YA MAY 'ROUSE
THEM THERE COWS!"

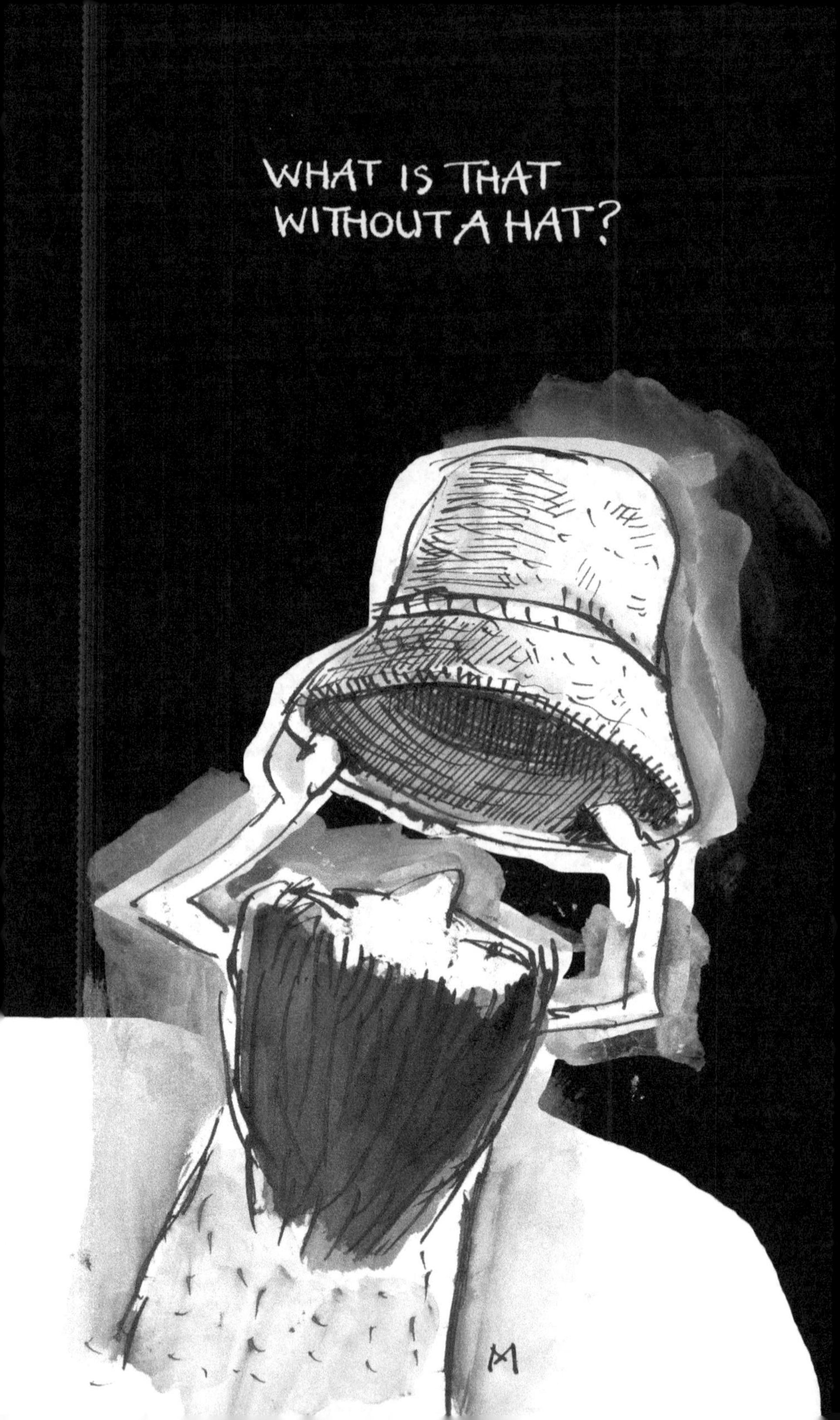

WHAT IS THAT
WITHOUT A HAT?

DOES A PRINCESS MISBEHAVED
DESERVE TO BE SAVED? MAYBE,
IF SHE'S HOLDING A BABY.

"I'M A HAS-BEEN
WITHOUT HUSBAND!"
STANDS A WIFE
WITH A KNIFE,
MID-LIFE.

POLYESTER HESTER HAS FORGOTTEN SHE AIN'T COTTON.
I MAY BE PLASTIC, BUT I'M FANTASTIC!

HER LUSH
MAKES HIM BLUSH,
HIS BLUSH
MAKES HER SMILE—
KAYLEE AND KYLE.

"I AM PURPLE.
WHO ARE YOU?"
"WE'RE YOUR PARENTS,
RED AND BLUE."

"I AM DENTIST MARY,
AND I'M A TOOTH-FAIRY.
I WILL GIVE YOU A RICH PRIZE
FOR THE TOOTH THAT TELLS LIES.
AND I WILL GRANT YOU ETERNAL YOUTH
FOR THE TOOTH THAT TELLS ONLY TRUTH.

THE EYES DO NOT FEAR
NEITHER LEFT NOR RIGHT EAR,
BUT THE TONGUE HIDES IN THE CAVE,
AND DOES HIS BEST TO BEHAVE.
BUT, ALAS—"YOU SILLY ASS!"
—SOME TIMES IT SLIPS,
AND EMBARASSES THE LIPS,
AND GETS CHASTISED BY THE TEETH,
LURKING 'BOVE AND BENEATH.

NOW THAT THE OLD GEEZER
SPAT OUT HIS DENTURES,
I'M SAFE TO PURSUE
MY OWN MISADVENTURES!

"I AM THE GREENEST
   YOU EVER SEENEST!"
   GLOATS THE GRASS ON THAT SIDE.
"AND I CAN GLADLY PROVIDE
INDISPUTABLE SCIENTIFIC PROOF
PERFORMED FROM A NEUTRAL ROOF."

"ONCE IN A WHILE
I CAN'T HELP BUT SMILE,"
ADMITS THE FROWN,
FEELING UPSIDE DOWN.

MACHETE BETTY

A WICKED, OLD TALE
GETS OUT OF JAIL.
BUT ONCE FREED,
IT REPEATS ITS DEED.

"DO NOT BE TOO RASH
TO THINK ME TRASH."
"BUT... I LOVE YOU, STAN,
AND I AM A GARBAGE CAN!"

MY ONLY DUTY
IS TO BEAUTY.

"I MAY LOVE YOU, BUT...
PFUUU....
...THEN AGAIN, I MAY NOT,"
CIGAR TELLS THE JAR.
BIZARRE.

"WHY DOES RELAXING
HAVE TO BE SO TAXING?
I AM NEARLY EXHAUSTED!"
HE LAMENTABLY BOASTED.

RECIPE IDEA

DEMENTED, SCENTED

PING PONG
KING KONG

"I WANNA BE YOUR MASCOT!"
PLEADS THE MAD CASKET.

TOILET PAPER CAPER

I AIN'T LIKIN' THAT VIKIN'!
"WOULD YA PLEASE STOP
WAVIN' YER AXE,
SIT DOWN, AND RELAX,
THIS 'ERE VILLAGE
AIN'T RIPE FOR PILLAGE.
SO, 'AVE SOME OF OUR BEER,
AN' COME BACK NEX' YEAR."

SLEEPING BEAUTY WOKE,
GLARED, AND SPOKE—
"WHO GAVE YOU CONSENT, SIR KENT?!
BENEATH THAT SHINY, SILVER SUIT,
YOU ARE NAUGHT
BUT A SWEATY, STINKY BRUTE!
A TOXIC BEAST
FROM NETHER REGIONS RELEASED!"

"WAIT, M'LADY, WAIT!
S'ME — LOOK!"
"HUH... WHAT?
IS THAT YOU, BIG BROOKE?
YOU LOOK AS OLD
AS DUST ON MOLD!
HOW LONG HAVE I BEEN ASLEEP?"
"M'LADY, 'TIS AS WELL
IF I DON'T TELL.
T'WOULD MAKE YE WEEP!"

IS THE KA-BOOM OF A CLOUD
A THOUGHT SPOKEN TOO LOUD?
M

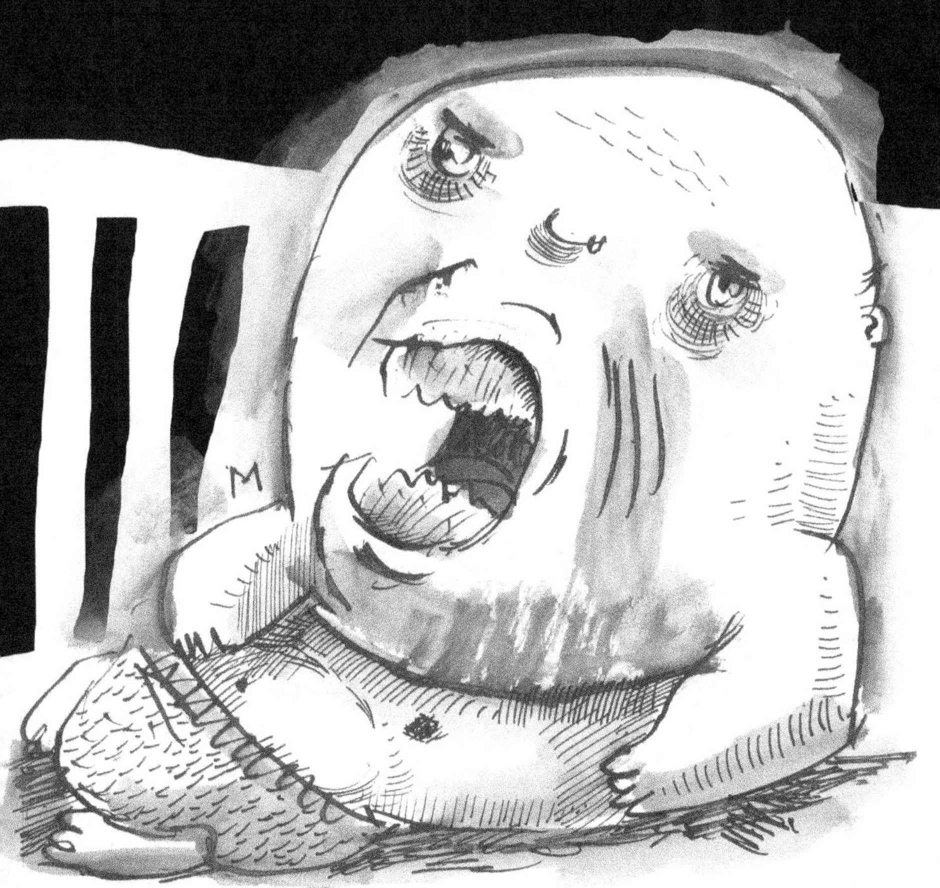

FIRST, HER BABY
ATE HER BREAST.
THEN HER BABY
ATE HER REST.
HMM..., MAYBE,
IT'S A ZOMBIE BABY!

RECIPE IDEA

STUFF A LAUGH
WITH 2 LIMES
AND 2 RHYMES

"OUCH!"
CRIES COUCH,
"MAY I SEE YOUR PERMIT
TO SIT?"
NO LOiTERiNG

CRACKED PEG,
THE FRESHLY BOILED EGG—
"I AM HOTTER
THAN HARRY POTTER!"

" I PROPOSE
TO PUT DENIAL ON TRIAL,"
SAYS TOM SAWYER,
TURNED AMBITIOUS LAWYER,
TO THE JUDGE WITH A SMUDGE
ON THE TIP OF HIS NOSE.

"I ORDER NOODLES, BUT YOU BRING ME TWO FAT OVERCOOKED POODLES!"
"MY SINCERE APOLOGIES, MONSIER, OUR CHEF IS HALF-DEAF."
oi, oi, oi, BOK CHOY! SPAM NO HAM...
...AN' POODLES AIN'T NOODLES!
M

A PAIR OF OLD THOUGHTS
POP OUT OF THE BOX—
"SURPRISE!"
—AND FLOAT UP TO THE SKIES.

"HOW DARE
YOU BE HAPPY
WHILE I'M SAD!"
YELLS BLAIRE, MAD.

"I'M A GONNA CHANGE DA WORL',"
SAYS THE LITTLE GIRL.
"WHEN I GWOW UP.
AN' I'M A STA'T WIT'CHOO,
POP!"

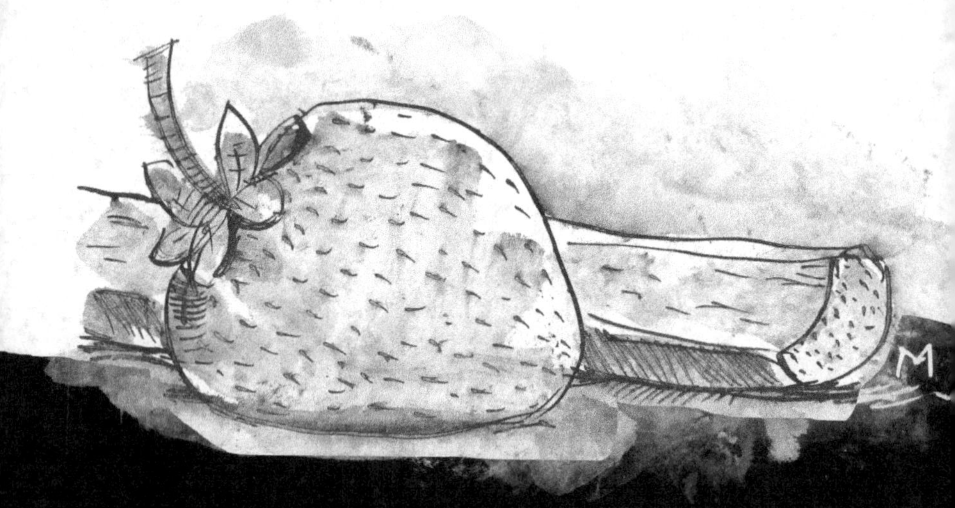

RHUBARB
WANTS TO MARRY
STRAWBERRY.
"ABSOLUTELY NOT! DON'T TALK ROT."
"BUT, MOTHER, WE LOVE EACH OTHER!
WE ARE SOUL MATES—
LIKE SWEET AN' SOUR,
LIKE EGGS AN' FLOUR,
LIKE MINUTE AN' HOUR..."
"I THOUGHT SWEET LOVED SPICY."
"NOT NO MORE! THAT WAS BEFORE,
BUT THINGS GOT STALE AN' ICY.
SWEET
FELT INCOMPLETE."

I HAVE A HUNCH
THAT BETTY BOOG
LOVES TO MUNCH
ON TOASTED BOOGERS FOR LUNCH.
"YES, YES, 'TIS TRUE!
I CALLS THEM MY 'WICKED CHEW'.
I DIPS THEM IN HONEY,
THEN SELLS THEM
TO EARN EXTRA MONEY,
AT MY LEMONADE STAND —
THE BETTY BOOG BOOGER BRAND,
I ATTEST IS THE BEST
IN THE PACIFIC NORTHWEST."

DO NOT BE DISTRAUGHT
BY YOUR OWN THOUGHT.
RATHER, THINK ANOTHER.
BUT DO AVOID THINKING
THAT THOUGHT'S BROTHER.

DO NOT MANHANDLE
A BURNING CANDLE.

I STAND ON THE BRINK
OF MY KITCHEN SINK
AND THINK — "OH, HECK,
THERE'S A RAT ON MY DECK,
EATING A POTATO
AND READING PLATO."

DETECTIVE CRUNCH
HAD A HUNCH
FOR LUNCH.

"MY FART
IS FINE ART,"
SAYS THE FARTIST FINE ARTIST,
WITH HIS NOSE UP IN THE AIR,
PRETENDING HE IS SOME
RARE HEIR.

"YOU BETTER BEHA-A-AVE, HENRY, YOU KNA-A-AVE!" COMES THE DISCORDANT VOICE FROM HIS GRANDFATHER'S GRAVE.

"I AM A SWAN!"
PROCLAIMS THE UGLY DUCKLING,
CHUCKLING.

"I DON'T WANT TO GLO-O-O-OAT,
BUT I'M THE BREEZIEST NO-O-O-OTE
ON THE SC-C-CALE,"
SINGS G#ALE.

I DON'T RESENTS
ANY O' ME DENTS—
I BIN SHOVED
AN' I BIN LOVED.

I SPOT MARK TWAIN
SIPPING CHAMPAGNE.
HE SAYS TOM SAWYER
IS NOW A BORING LAWYER,
AND HUCK FINN
NOW LIVES IN BERLIN
WITH BEER BELLY
AND DOUBLE CHIN.

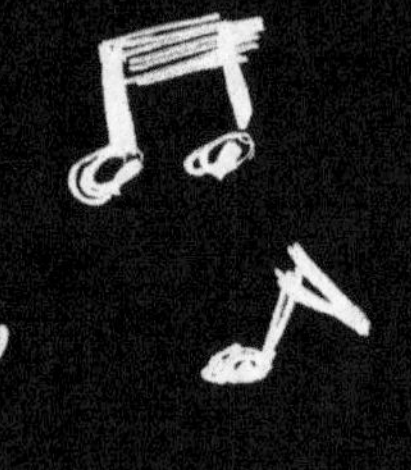

WHILE FLOATING IN A BLUE BALLOON,
ABOVE A TRACT OF THISTLES,
TO HERSELF, A LAUGING ELF,
A TICKLING TUNE A'WHISTLES...

A KITTEN, MOST FOUL,
MEOW MEOW,
IS ON THE PROWL,
MEOW MEOW,
IN KRAKOW-OW-OW,
MEOW MEOW

THE STREETS ARE DESERTED,
THE POPE'S BEEN ALERTED,
PANIC AND FEAR HAS GRIPPED—
POOR POLISH PEOPLE HAVE FLIPPED!
THE KITTEN IS HUNTING FOR CHOW,
MEOW MEOW-OW-OW-OWWww

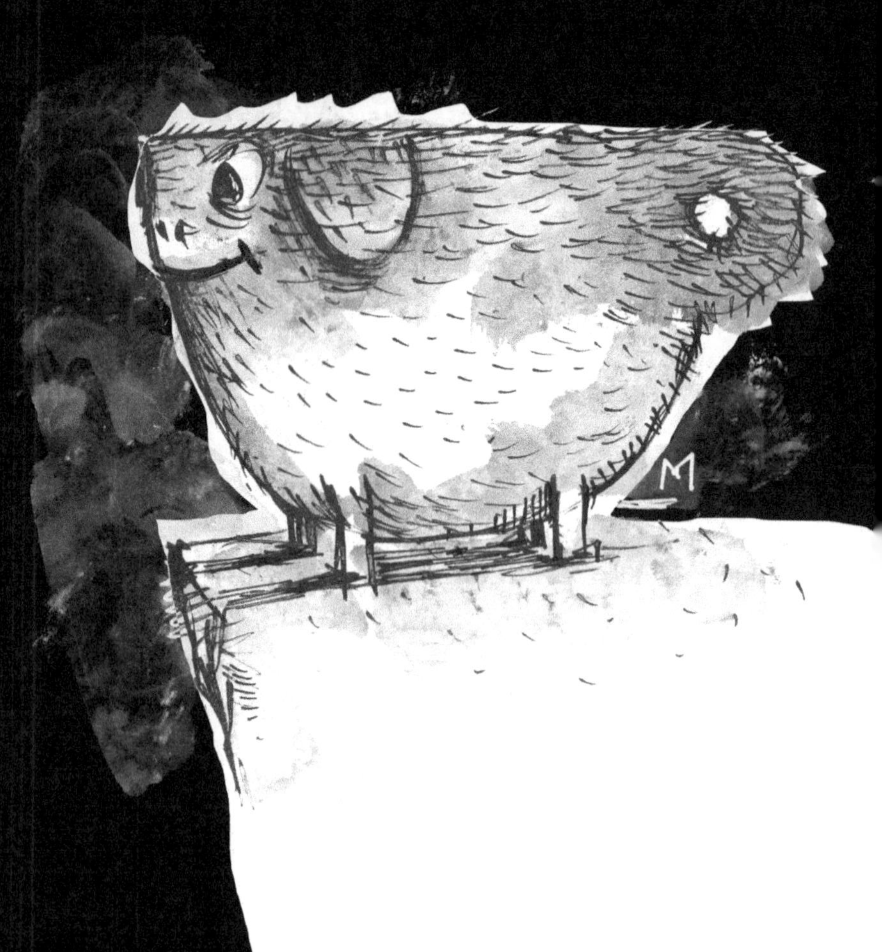

WHAT IF
I LEAPT OFF A CLIFF
INTO TEA,
WOULD MY FLEAS
FOLLOW ME?

"I AM THE QUEEN
OF SERENE,"
PROCLAIMS GRASS
ON THE PLATEAU.
"IF YOU WANT TO UNWIND,
AND YOU ISN'T BLIND,
GRAB SNACKS, RELAX,
AND WATCH ME GROW."

CALL THE POLICE!
CALL THE POLICE!
I MADE ME
A MONSTERPIECE!

"I WILL NOT ALLOW IT!"
WAILS WILLIE'S WALLET.

I WANT TO B SINGLE
TO MINGLE WITH OTHERS
LIKE ME. BUT, INSTEAD,
I AM STUCK INSIDE
THIS DE RIS
FAMILY

LETTE S
I FETTE S
REAK OUT AND SHOUT,
BUT NO ONE NDER TANDS
WHA BOUT.

M

T

A

U

B

R R

N

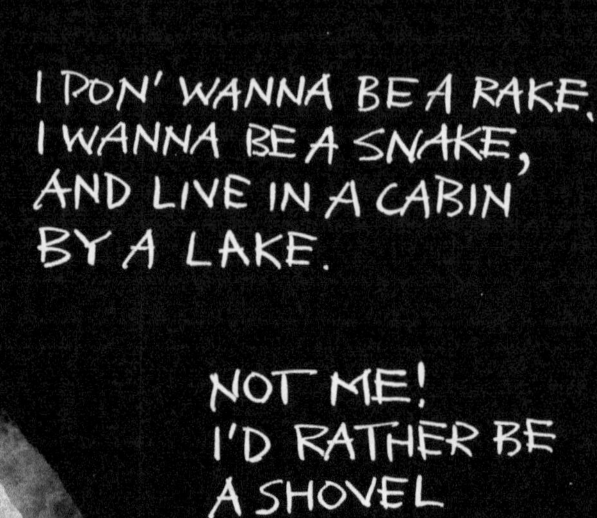

I DON' WANNA BE A RAKE.
I WANNA BE A SNAKE,
AND LIVE IN A CABIN
BY A LAKE.

NOT ME!
I'D RATHER BE
A SHOVEL
AND LIVE
IN A HOVEL.

WHO KNOWS, WHO KNOWS,
IF THESE BE FINGERS,
OR TOES?

FIRST, DAISY DENIES.
THEN, SHE CRIES.
JUST LOOK AT THE SIZE
OF THOSE SAD, WATERY
EYES!
THAT EYE
IS BETTER.
IT LOOKS
WETTER!
IT AIN'T THE SEA,
BUT IT'S SALTY ENOUGH
FOR ME.

I LIKE MY BABIES WIT'OUT RABIES!
DON'T HAVE A SHIVER, MAN UP AND DELIVER,

I GOT A THOUGHT. IT IS FINE.
YOU CAN'T HAVE MY THOUGHT—
IT IS MINE, MINE,
ALL MINE!

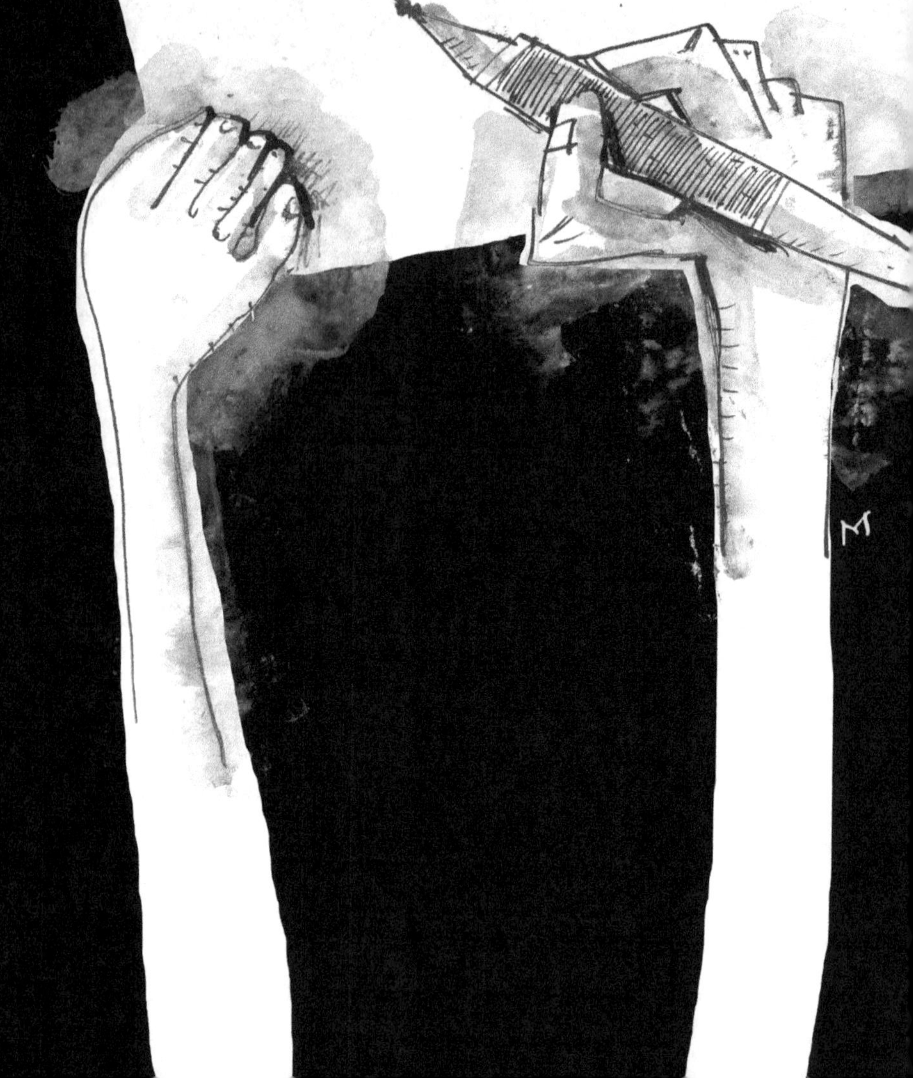

HAIL, HAIL,
DEAR ABIGAIL,
CAN B-ING Z CLEVER
RUIN AN ENDEAVOR?
THANKS A BANKS,
TREMULOUS TREVOR

DEAR TR-R-R-REMULOUS,
YES! TRYING 2 IMPRESS
WILL MAKE U SEEM LESS,
AND BEING 2 SLY
WON'T GET U NIGH
2 THAT LITHE LASS
IN U'R LIT CLASS.
A RUM WELCOME,
HOLY GRAIL
ABIGAIL

"ART,
YOU GOT A HEART
OF STEEL!" "BUT, LUCILLE,
I AM AN AUTOMOBILE!"

MISS,
MY NAME IS DOUG.
I DON'T WANT A KISS,
BUT I'D LIKE A HUG.

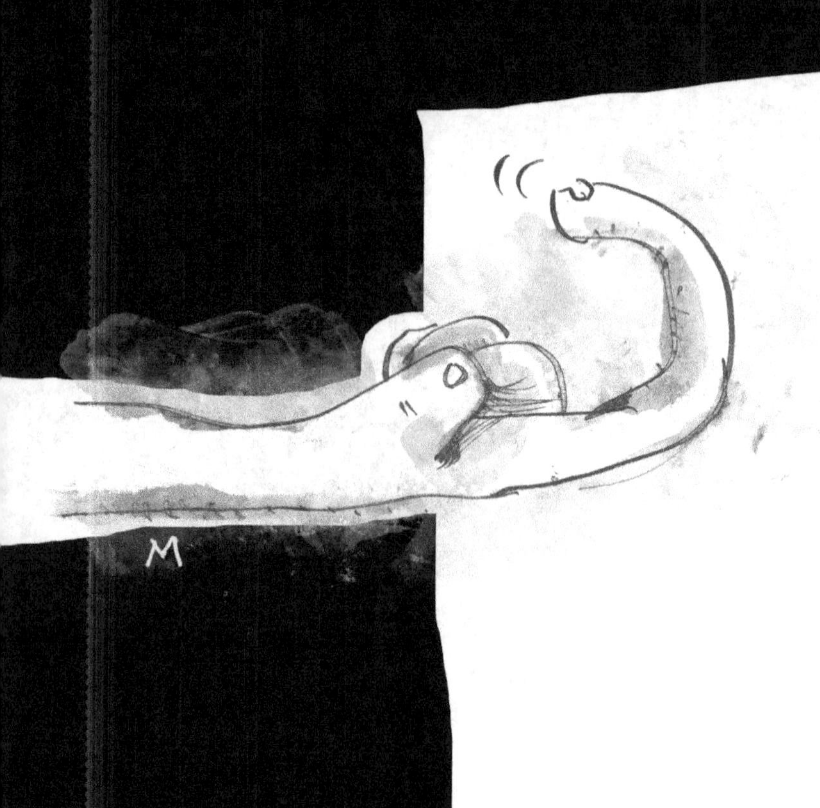

"I WANT MORE POWER!"
HOLLERS HALF-HOUR,
AND SLYLY BECKONS
SIX INNOCENT SECONDS.
M

BE HOLD!
MOLD!
$OLD

NEVER!

WHATEVER
FOR?

THAT'S
WHEN
ADORE
TURNS
TO CHORE,

AND
EACH
HOUR
TURNS
SOUR.

M

STEVE STOLE A STOVE —
"BUT, YOUR HONOR,
I DID IT FOR LOVE!"

" 'TILL DEATH DO US PART—
IS THAT SMART?

NEVER MIND! NEVER MIND!
I WILL FIND MY HAPPY
WITH ANOTHER CHAPPIE.

WHEN YOUR THOUGHTS FIGHT,
HOW DO YOU DECIDE
WHICH THOUGHT IS RIGHT,
WHICH IS THE WINNER—
"MOM, WHAT'S FOR DINNER?"
—WHICH IS FULL,
WHICH HOLLOW,
AND WHICH IS BEST
TO FOLLOW?

DON'T LET YOUR THOUGHTS
SAFELY NESTLE.
LET THEM WRESTLE.
TOO MUCH PEACE IN YOUR MIND
CAN LEAVE YOU WEAK
AND CONFINED.

M

SO LET US NOW PAUSE
FOR A SILENT APPLAUSE...

SURELY THIS,
MY FRIENDS,
THE END
PORTENDS

DON'T MOPE,
YOU DOPE,
HAVE SOME GUILE
AND DARE
TO SMILE.

SHE WAS FIRST,
BUT THEN REVERSED.

THE
END

"YOU STAND BEFORE ME BEMUSED,
BUT YOU HAVE BEEN PROPERLY ACCUSED
OF DOING CRIME
BY WRITING...AHEM... RIDICULOUS RHYME!
MISTER O'CONNER,
HOW DO YOU PLEAD?"
"I'M GUILTY, YOUR HONOR,
GUILTY, INDEED!"
"WELL, THEN, I HOPE
THIS HERE SENTENCE
BRINGS ON YOUR FULL REPENTANCE."
"IT WILL. IT WILL. IT ALREADY HAS!"
NO NEED TO LOCK ME IN ALCATRAZ.
I'M DONE WITH RHYME. DONE!
(I'VE TAKEN UP JAZZ.)"

I HAVE BEEN MISCAST
BY BEING PLACED LAST.
I AM NOT A KEY.
I AM NOT A SAGE.
I DON'T WANT TO BE
THE END PAGE.

www.ingramcontent.com/pod-product-compliance
Lightning Source LLC
Chambersburg PA
CBHW070507160726
48003CB00004B/1467